DC

STICKER ART PUZZLES

CLASSIC COMIC BOOK COVERS

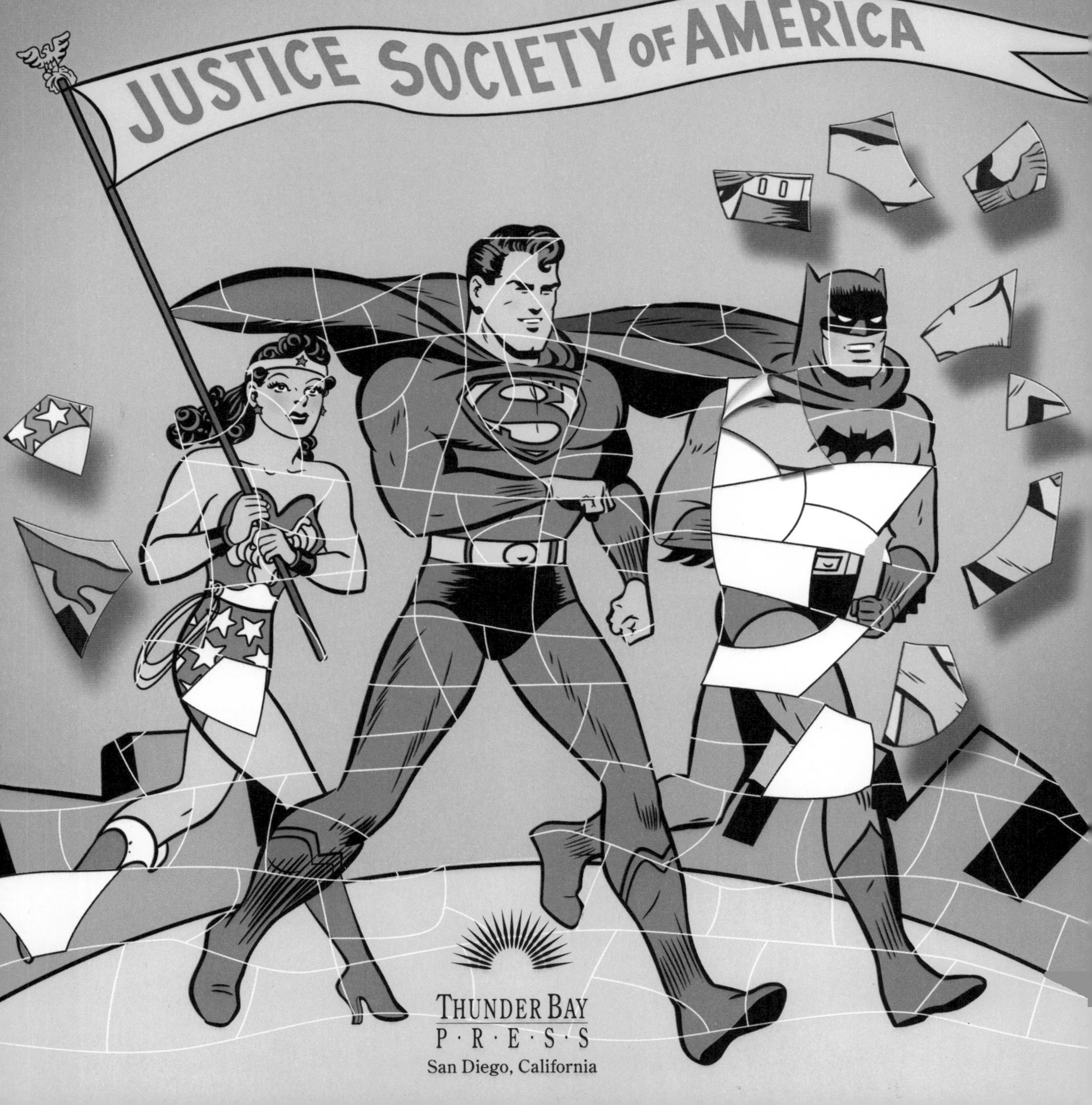
JUSTICE SOCIETY OF AMERICA

THUNDER BAY
P·R·E·S·S
San Diego, California

Thunder Bay Press
An imprint of Printers Row Publishing Group
9717 Pacific Heights Blvd., San Diego, CA 92121
www.thunderbaybooks.com • mail@thunderbaybooks.com

Printers Row Publishing Group is a division of Readerlink Distribution Services, LLC.
Thunder Bay Press is a registered trademark of Readerlink Distribution Services, LLC.

Correspondence regarding the content of this book should be sent to Thunder Bay Press, Editorial
Department, at the above address.

Thunder Bay Press
Publisher: Peter Norton
Associate Publisher: Ana Parker
Senior Developmental Editor: Diane Cain
Editor: Jessica Matteson
Production Team: Rusty von Dyl, Mimi Oey, Beno Chan

Produced by Judy O Productions, Inc.
Author: Steve Behling

ISBN: 978-1-68412-893-8

Printed, manufactured, and assembled in Dongguan, China

25 24 23 22 21   1 2 3 4 5

CONTENTS

INTRODUCTION

FROM THE FIRST APPEARANCE OF SUPERMAN IN 1938, THE DC SUPER HEROES WOULD TAKE THE WORLD BY STORM. CHARACTERS LIKE BATMAN AND WONDER WOMAN CAPTURED THE POPULAR IMAGINATION. THE FLASH, GREEN LANTERN, AND SUPERGIRL HAVE ALL BECOME HOUSEHOLD NAMES, EASILY IDENTIFIED BY CHILD AND ADULT ALIKE.

THROUGH THE GOLDEN AGE OF COMICS (1938-1956) INTO THE SILVER AGE (1956-1970), DC LED THE WAY WITH DARING ADVENTURES FEATURING THE MOST ICONIC SUPER HEROES THE WORLD HAD EVER SEEN.

ON THESE PAGES YOU'LL FIND FIFTEEN STUNNING VINTAGE COMIC BOOK STICKER PUZZLES FEATURING YOUR FAVORITE DC SUPER HEROES AND SUPER-VILLAINS. WITH MORE THAN ONE HUNDRED STICKERS PER PUZZLE, YOU'LL BECOME YOUR OWN HERO AS YOU PIECE TOGETHER CLASSIC COVERS, CREATED BY AN ARRAY OF AMAZINGLY TALENTED ARTISTS FROM COMICS HISTORY. YOU'LL ALSO DISCOVER FASCINATING FACTS ABOUT THE CHARACTERS, AS WELL AS HISTORICAL INFORMATION ABOUT THE COMICS.

GET READY FOR HOURS OF FUN AS YOU PIECE TOGETHER THESE PUZZLES TO SEE VINTAGE DC COMICS COVERS APPEAR BEFORE YOUR EYES.

GET OUT THERE, HERO!

INSTRUCTIONS

ON EACH PUZZLE PAGE, YOU'LL FIND A GRID. USE THE STICKERS TO REVEAL ICONIC SUPER HEROES AND SUPER-VILLAINS ON HISTORIC COMIC BOOK COVERS FROM THE DC UNIVERSE.

HOW TO SOLVE THE PUZZLES

EACH STICKER PUZZLE FEATURES A FRAMED "OUTLINE" OF THE COMIC BOOK COVER YOU WILL PIECE TOGETHER. ENCLOSED IN THE OUTLINE ARE GEOMETRIC SPACES THAT OFFER HINTS WHERE EACH PIECE GOES. APPLY EACH STICKER TO ITS CORRESPONDING SHAPE IN THE OUTLINE. THE STICKERS CAN BE MOVED IN CASE YOU MAKE A MISTAKE. USE YOUR SUPER POWERS TO WORK YOUR WAY THROUGH THE PUZZLES!

THE STICKERS START ON PAGE 52. ALL OF THE PAGES IN THE BOOK ARE PERFORATED, SO YOU CAN TEAR OUT THE PUZZLE, STICKERS, AND SOLUTIONS PAGE TO LAY THEM ALL OUT AS YOU WORK. YOU CAN SOLVE THE PUZZLES SOLO OR ROUND UP YOUR SUPER HERO TEAM AND EACH TACKLE A PUZZLE. IF YOU NEED A LITTLE HELP, NUMBERED SOLUTIONS BEGIN ON PAGE 36, OR USE THE PUZZLE KEY ON THE BACK FLAP FOR REFERENCE.

PUZZLES

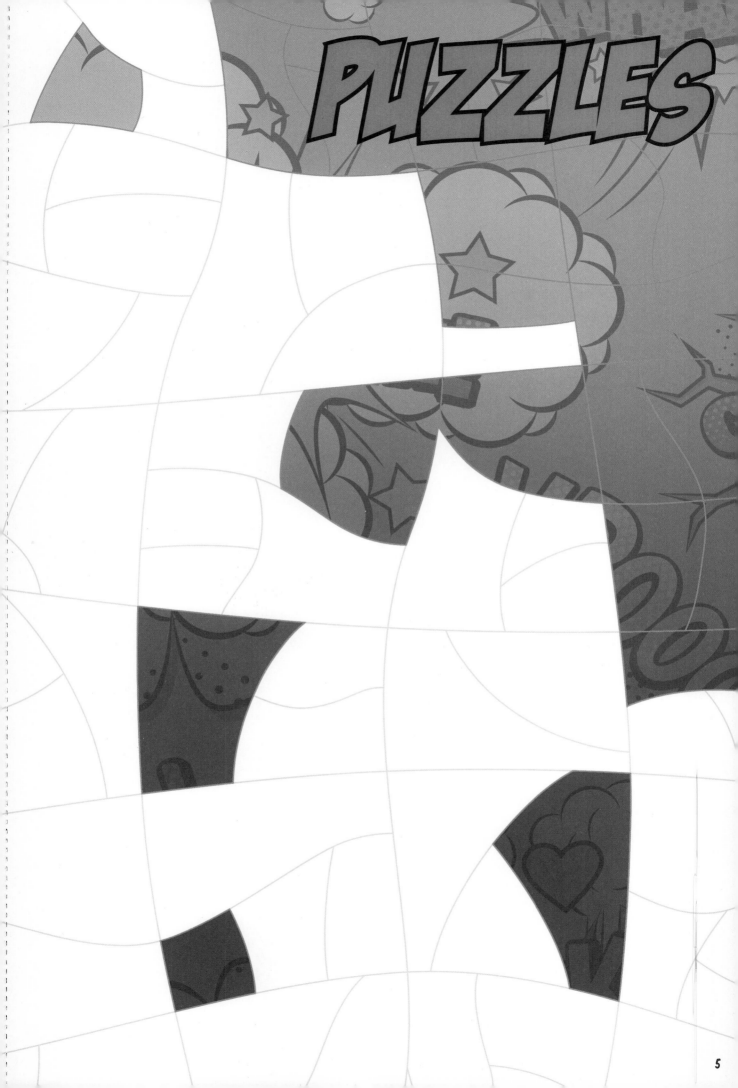

Wonder Woman™

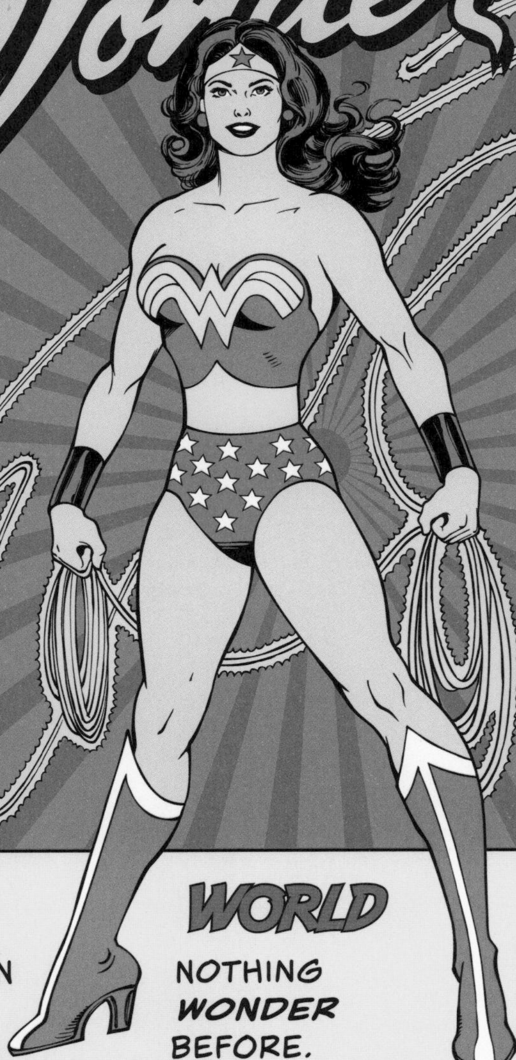

THE WORLD HAD SEEN NOTHING LIKE ***WONDER WOMAN*** BEFORE. HAILING FROM PARADISE ISLAND, WHICH LATER BECAME KNOWN AS THEMYSCIRA, PRINCESS DIANA LIVED WITH HER AMAZON SISTERS IN *PEACE* AND *HARMONY*, REMOVED FROM THE WORLD OF MAN. UNDER THE BENEVOLENT RULE OF HER MOTHER, QUEEN HIPPOLYTA, THE AMAZONS HAD SPENT CENTURIES PERFECTING THEMSELVES BOTH ***PHYSICALLY*** AND ***MENTALLY***.

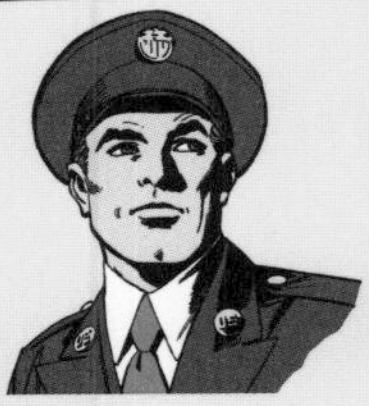

WHEN U.S. INTELLIGENCE OFFICER *STEVE TREVOR* CRASH-LANDED ON THE REMOTE ISLAND DURING THE DARK DAYS OF WORLD WAR II, HIPPOLYTA DECREED THAT ONE OF THE AMAZONS MUST RETURN HIM TO "MAN'S WORLD."

A COMPETITION ENSUED, ONE FROM WHICH DIANA WAS *STRICTLY FORBIDDEN* TO PARTICIPATE. DONNING A DISGUISE, DIANA NOT ONLY TOOK PART IN THE CONTEST, BUT *SHE WON.*

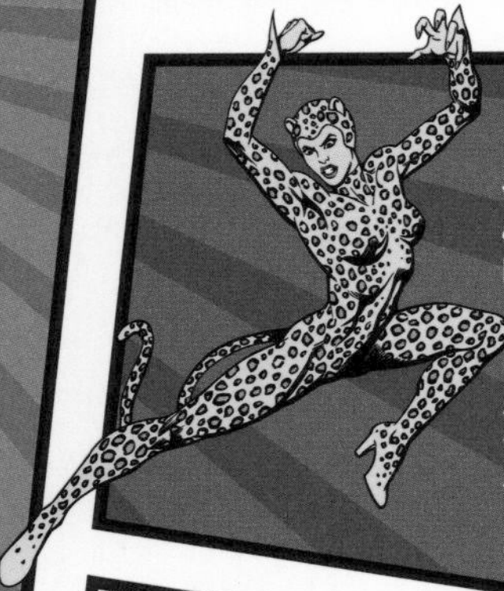

ARRIVING IN THE UNITED STATES, *PRINCESS DIANA* FOUND HERSELF DUBBED *WONDER WOMAN* AS SHE FOUGHT ALONGSIDE STEVE TO STOP THE NAZIS, AS WELL AS *SINISTER FOES* THE CHEETAH, DOCTOR POISON, AND GIGANTA.

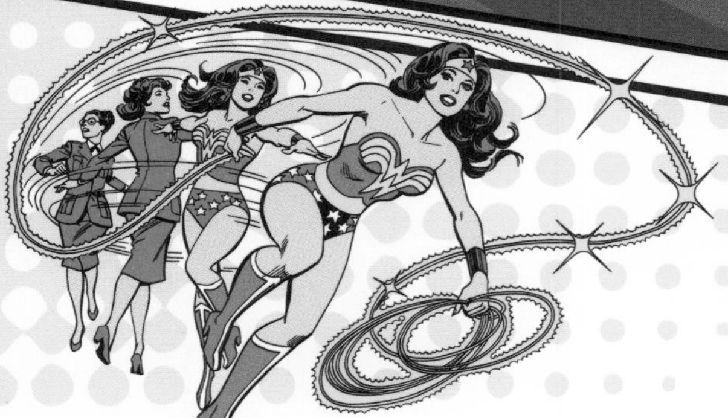

IN THE STORY "WONDER WOMAN ARRIVES IN MAN'S WORLD," FEATURED IN ***SENSATION COMICS #1***, OUR HERO ENCOUNTERS A NURSE WITH THE NAME DIANA PRINCE, WHO HAPPENS TO BE A ***DEAD RINGER*** FOR THE AMAZON. TAKING THE NURSE'S IDENTITY, DIANA BECOMES THE NURSE TO ***STEVE TREVOR***, STILL RECOVERING FROM HIS PLANE CRASH, AND CHASES DOWN A ***NAZI SPY RING***.

ALTHOUGH SENSATION COMICS #1 MARKED THE FIRST TIME WONDER WOMAN APPEARED ON A COMIC BOOK COVER, SHE MADE HER DEBUT THREE MONTHS EARLIER IN THE PAGES OF ***ALL-STAR COMICS #8***, *PUBLISHED IN OCTOBER 1941.*

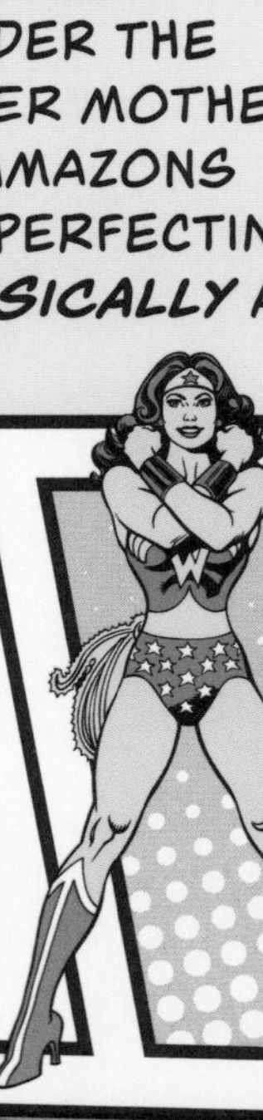

THE GOLDEN AGE WONDER WOMAN WAS A MEMBER OF THE JUSTICE SOCIETY, WHILE HER SILVER AGE INCARNATION WAS A MEMBER OF THE ***JUSTICE LEAGUE OF AMERICA***.

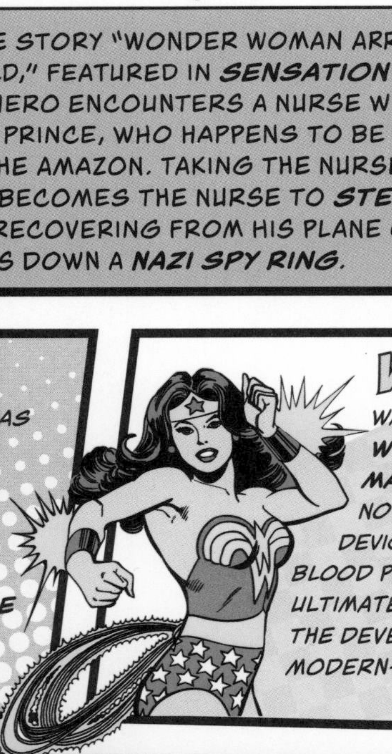

WONDER WOMAN WAS CREATED BY ***WILLIAM MOULTON MARSTON***, *WHO ALSO NOTABLY DEVELOPED A DEVICE FOR MEASURING BLOOD PRESSURE, WHICH ULTIMATELY FIGURED INTO THE DEVELOPMENT OF THE MODERN-DAY LIE DETECTOR.*

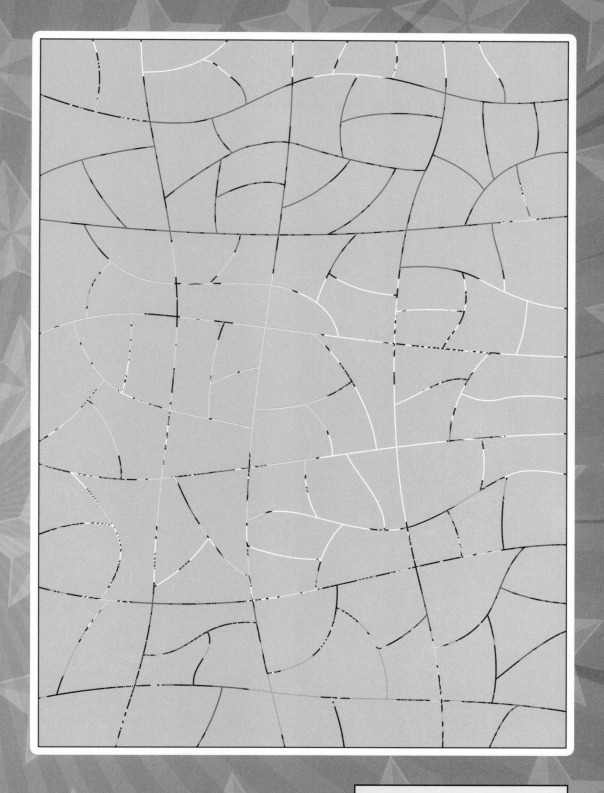

SENSATION COMICS #1
JANUARY 1942
ART BY HARRY G. PETER

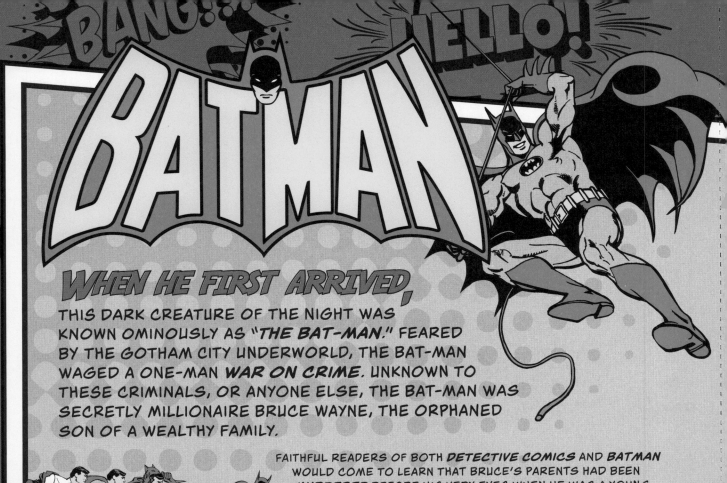

BATMAN

WHEN HE FIRST ARRIVED,

THIS DARK CREATURE OF THE NIGHT WAS KNOWN OMINOUSLY AS "*THE BAT-MAN*." FEARED BY THE GOTHAM CITY UNDERWORLD, THE BAT-MAN WAGED A ONE-MAN ***WAR ON CRIME***. UNKNOWN TO THESE CRIMINALS, OR ANYONE ELSE, THE BAT-MAN WAS SECRETLY MILLIONAIRE BRUCE WAYNE, THE ORPHANED SON OF A WEALTHY FAMILY.

FAITHFUL READERS OF BOTH ***DETECTIVE COMICS*** AND ***BATMAN*** WOULD COME TO LEARN THAT BRUCE'S PARENTS HAD BEEN ***MURDERED*** BEFORE HIS VERY EYES WHEN HE WAS A YOUNG CHILD. THAT MOMENT WAS SEARED INTO BRUCE'S MEMORY, AND HE ***SWORE VENGEANCE*** AGAINST ALL CRIMINALS. HE SPENT THE ENSUING YEARS STUDYING CRIMINOLOGY AND SCIENCE, ALL THE WHILE BECOMING A MASTER OF MARTIAL ARTS AND VARIOUS FORMS OF ARMED AND UNARMED COMBAT.

OVER TIME, HE WOULD BECOME KNOWN AS SIMPLY BATMAN AND ACQUIRE A PARTNER IN DICK GRAYSON, A.K.A. ***ROBIN THE BOY WONDER***. HE WOULD ALSO CULTIVATE A STAGGERING ***ROGUES GALLERY*** OF COLORFUL FOES, INCLUDING THE PENGUIN, CATWOMAN, RIDDLER, AND THE INFAMOUS ***JOKER***.

ISSUE #33 OF ***DETECTIVE COMICS*** FEATURED A FLASHBACK TO THE MOMENT WHEN BRUCE'S PARENTS, THOMAS AND MARTHA WAYNE, WERE ***GUNNED DOWN*** BY AN UNNAMED ASSAILANT. BRUCE DREW INSPIRATION FROM THE BAT TO BECOME A ***DARK KNIGHT OF JUSTICE***. HE THEN WENT ON TO FACE THE MENACE OF THE SCARLET HORDE, UNDER THE COMMAND OF THE DASTARDLY DOCTOR CARL KRUGER.

ISSUE #33 OF DETECTIVE COMICS ALSO INCLUDED BACKUP FEATURES STARRING OTHER HEROES, AS WAS CUSTOMARY IN COMICS PUBLISHING AT THE TIME. READERS COULD THRILL TO "BART REGAN, SPY," "LARRY STEELE, PRIVATE DETECTIVE," AND THE WESTERN "BUCK MARSHALL."

BATMAN WAS CREATED BY ARTIST BOB KANE WITH WRITER BILL FINGER. THEY TOOK INSPIRATION FROM THE PULP HEROES OF THE DAY, INCLUDING THE SHADOW AND DOC SAVAGE. KANE WAS ALSO INSPIRED BY A DRAWING THAT ARTIST AND INVENTOR LEONARDO DA VINCI HAD DONE FEATURING A FLYING MACHINE WITH NOTABLY BAT-LIKE WINGS.

No. 27
64 PAGES OF ACTION!
MAY, 1939
Detective
COMICS
10¢

BATMAN MADE HIS FIRST APPEARANCE IN ***DETECTIVE COMICS #27*** (MAY 1939) IN "THE CASE OF THE CHEMICAL SYNDICATE." THE ISSUE IS ALSO THE INTRODUCTION OF A CHARACTER THAT WOULD BECOME A PILLAR OF THE BATMAN MYTHOS, ***COMMISSIONER GORDON***.

BATMAN / STICKERS ON PAGE 56. SOLUTION ON PAGE 38.

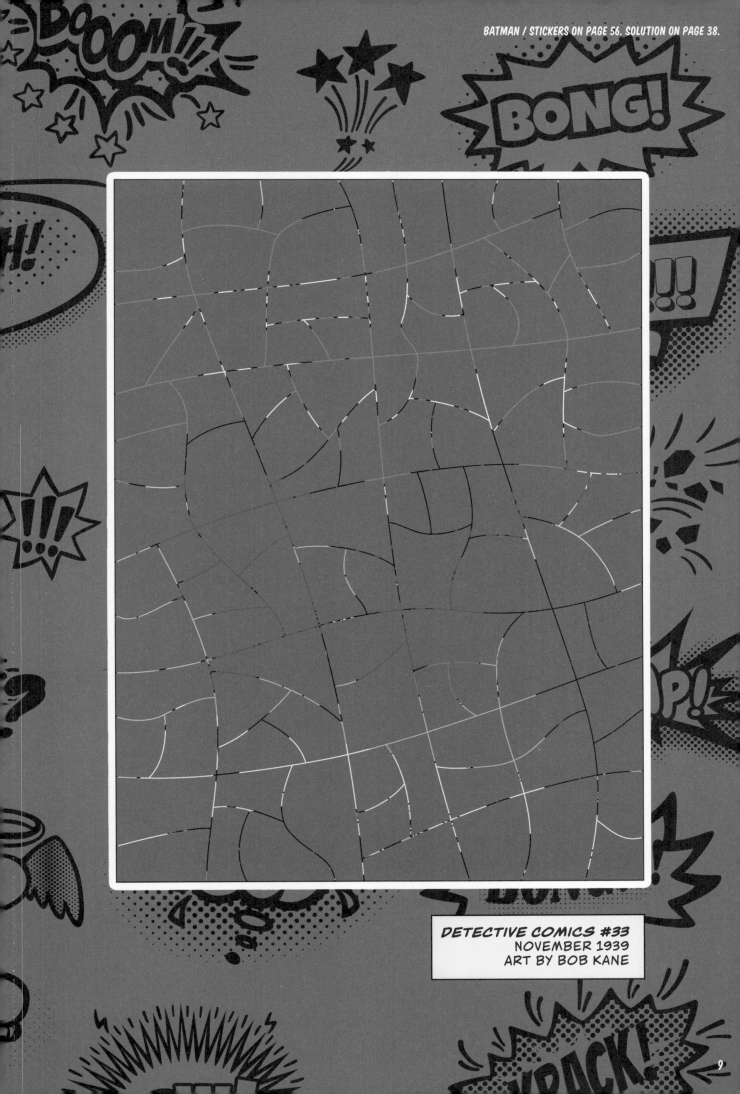

DETECTIVE COMICS #33
NOVEMBER 1939
ART BY BOB KANE

SUPERMAN™

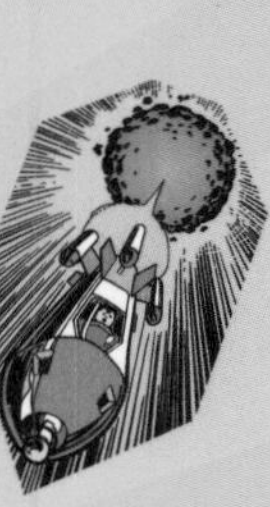

A STRANGE VISITOR

FROM ANOTHER PLANET, THE BABY ***KAL-EL*** WAS WHISKED AWAY VIA ROCKET FROM HIS HOME PLANET OF KRYPTON ONLY ***MOMENTS BEFORE ITS DESTRUCTION.*** THE INFANT SURVIVED THE TRIP, LANDING ON THE PLANET EARTH. TAKEN IN BY THE ELDERLY FARMERS JONATHAN AND MARTHA KENT, KAL-EL WOULD BE GIVEN AN EARTH NAME--CLARK KENT--AND THEN RAISED BY THE KENTS AS THEIR OWN FLESH AND BLOOD.

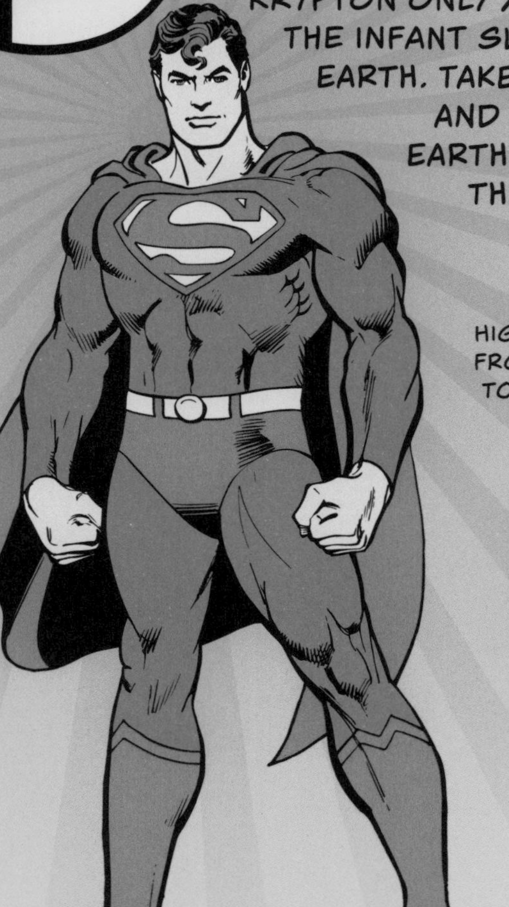

ALMOST IMMEDIATELY, IT BECAME APPARENT THAT THE CHILD HAD POWERS BEYOND COMPARE. HE WAS INCREDIBLY STRONG, REMARKABLY FAST, AND COULD LEAP HIGH INTO THE AIR. THESE ABILITIES SET YOUNG CLARK APART FROM HIS PEERS, AND HE WAS ADVISED BY HIS FOSTER FAMILY TO USE THOSE POWERS FOR THE BENEFIT OF ALL HUMANKIND.

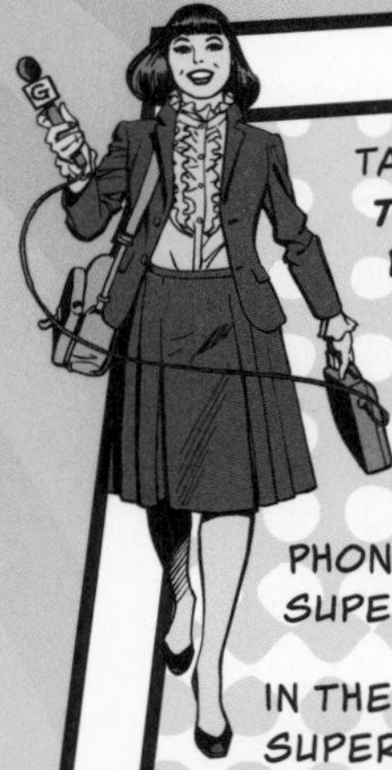

TAKING A POSITION AS REPORTER WITH ***THE DAILY PLANET*** NEWSPAPER IN THE BUSTLING CITY OF METROPOLIS, CLARK WORKED ALONGSIDE THE BRILLIANT ***LOIS LANE***, PHOTOGRAPHER ***JIMMY OLSEN***, AND EDITOR ***PERRY WHITE***. AND WHEN DANGER REARED ITS UGLY HEAD, CLARK WOULD DUCK INTO A SUPPLY CLOSET OR PHONE BOOTH AND EMERGE AS THE COSTUMED SUPERMAN--***THE MAN OF STEEL***.

IN THE PAGES OF ***ACTION COMICS #23***, SUPERMAN FIRST ENCOUNTERED THE FOE WHO WOULD CHALLENGE HIM THROUGHOUT THE DECADES, AGAIN AND AGAIN: ***LEX LUTHOR***. REFERRED TO ONLY BY HIS SURNAME IN THIS STORY, LUTHOR TRIED TO PROVOKE A WAR BETWEEN TWO COUNTRIES FROM THE SAFETY OF HIS DIRIGIBLE HIDEOUT.

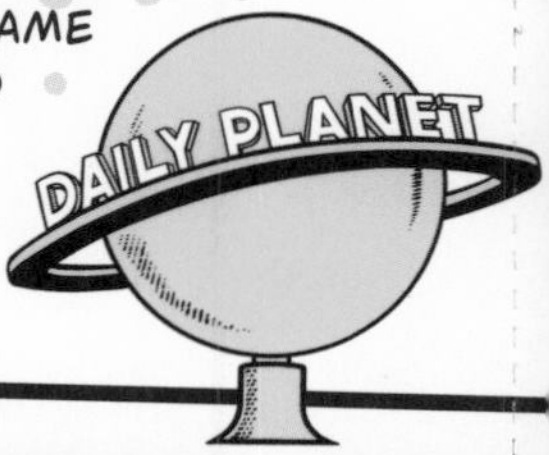
DAILY PLANET

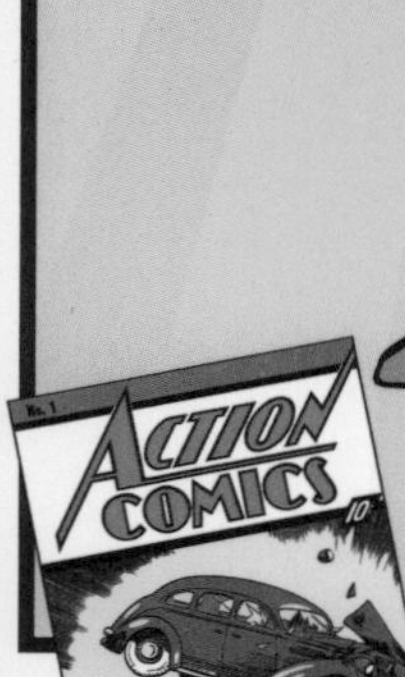
ACTION COMICS

SUPERMAN MADE HIS FIRST APPEARANCE IN ***ACTION COMICS #1*** (JUNE 1938), CREATED BY ***JERRY SIEGEL*** AND ***JOE SHUSTER***. THIS ISSUE FEATURED THE FIRST-EVER ORIGIN OF THE ***MAN OF STEEL***, AS WELL AS THE INTRODUCTION OF LOIS LANE. CURIOUSLY, BOTH SHE AND CLARK WORKED FOR NOT THE ***DAILY PLANET*** BUT THE ***DAILY STAR***!

LESS THAN TWO YEARS AFTER SUPERMAN APPEARED, THE CHARACTER MADE THE LEAP TO RADIO. ***THE ADVENTURES OF SUPERMAN*** RAN FROM 1940 UNTIL 1951, FEATURING ACTOR ***BUD COLLYER*** AS THE VOICE OF SUPERMAN. COLLYER WOULD REPRISE THE VOICE ROLE IN THE 1966 ANIMATED SERIES ***THE NEW ADVENTURES OF SUPERMAN***.

WHEN WE FIRST MEET SUPERMAN, HE IS ABLE TO ***LEAP BUILDINGS IN A SINGLE BOUND***--AND THAT'S ALL! THE FLYING WOULDN'T COME UNTIL ***THE ADVENTURES OF SUPERMAN*** RADIO SERIES, WHICH FEATURED THE INTRODUCTION: "LOOK! UP IN THE SKY! IT'S A BIRD! IT'S A PLANE! ***IT'S SUPERMAN!***"

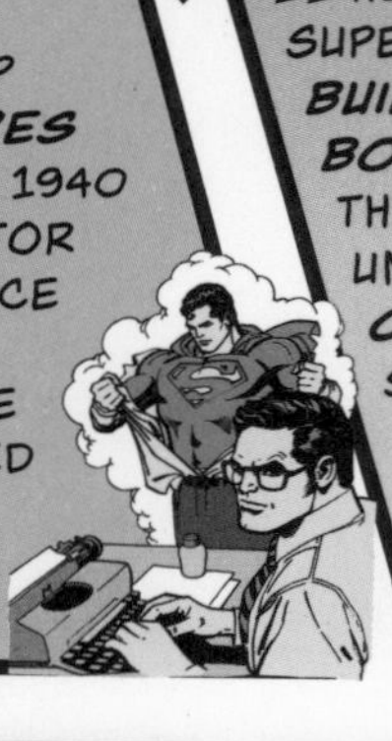

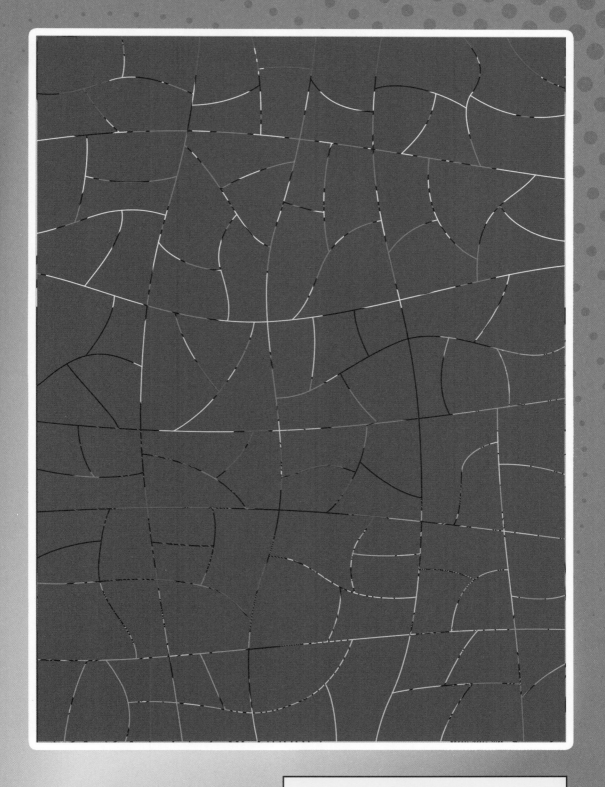

ACTION COMICS #23
APRIL 1940
ART BY JOE SHUSTER, PAUL CASSIDY

ROBIN

-THE BOY WONDER-

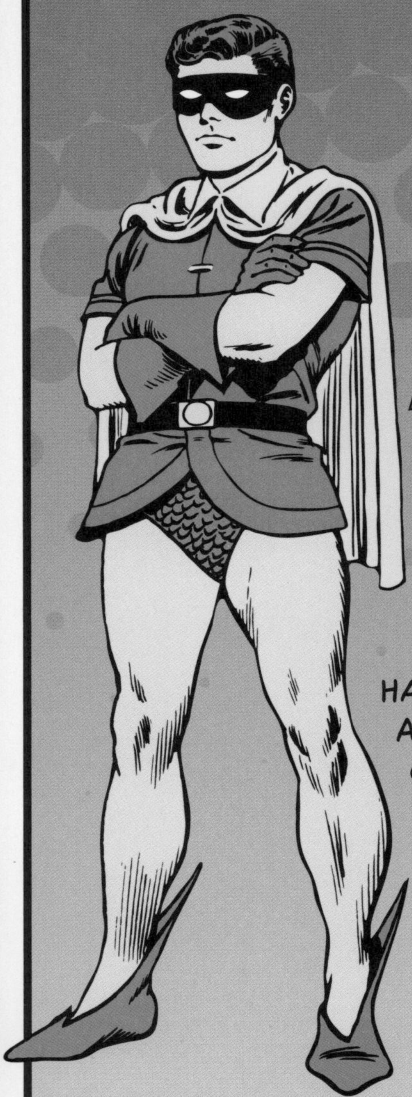

IT'S HARD TO IMAGINE BATMAN WITHOUT ROBIN. BUT THE DARK KNIGHT SPENT THE FIRST TWO YEARS OF HIS CAREER AS A SOLO ACT, HAUNTING THE STREETS AND ALLEYWAYS OF GOTHAM CITY IN PURSUIT OF EVIL. IT WASN'T UNTIL A TERRIBLE FATE BEFELL THE GRAYSON FAMILY THAT BRUCE WAYNE WOULD FIND A PARTNER IN HIS WAR ON CRIME.

THE FLYING GRAYSONS WERE A TRAPEZE ACT FOR A TRAVELING CIRCUS. THE CIRCUS OWNER, MR. HALY, WAS BEING SHAKEN DOWN BY LOCAL GANGSTERS UNDER THE EMPLOY OF BOSS ZUCCO, BUT HE REFUSED TO PAY. ZUCCO ORDERED HIS HIRED THUG, BLADE, TO KILL THE POPULAR FAMILY ACT THE FLYING GRAYSONS WHILE PERFORMING THAT VERY NIGHT. YOUNG DICK GRAYSON, THE SON OF THE FLYING GRAYSONS, WITNESSED THEIR FATE AND SWORE REVENGE UPON THE CRIMINALS RESPONSIBLE.

FATEFULLY, BRUCE WAS IN THE AUDIENCE THAT NIGHT AND TOOK IN THE NOW-ORPHANED ***DICK GRAYSON*** AS HIS WARD. HE TRAINED THE BOY, JUST AS HE HAD TRAINED HIMSELF, AND IN TIME, THE YOUTH WAS GIVEN HIS OWN COSTUMED IDENTITY, ***ROBIN***. TOGETHER, THEY WOULD GO AFTER BOSS ZUCCO, GATHERING EVIDENCE LEADING TO HIS ***ARREST AND CONVICTION***.

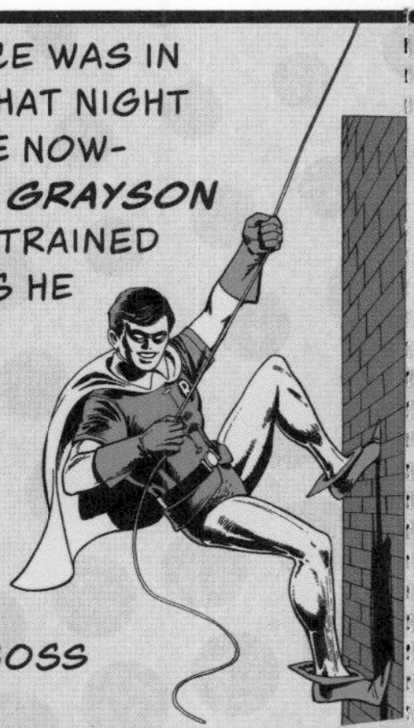

ISSUE #38 OF ***DETECTIVE COMICS*** SHOWCASED ROBIN'S EFFECTIVENESS AS A ***YOUNG CRIME FIGHTER***, HIS SKILL IN USING UNUSUAL WEAPONS (SUCH AS A SLINGSHOT), AND HIS PASSION FOR BRINGING ***CRIMINALS*** TO ***JUSTICE***.

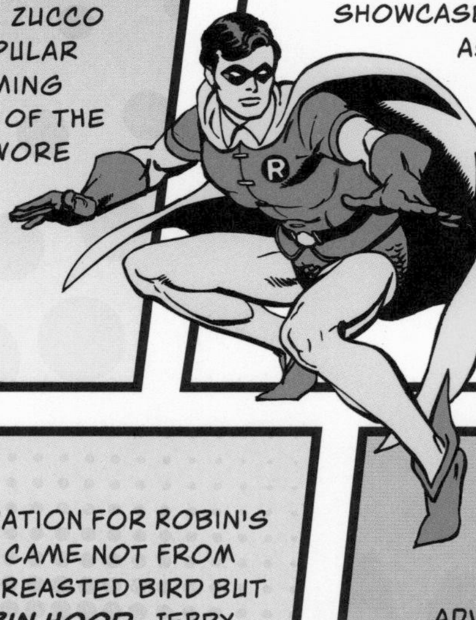

™

ROBIN PROVED TO BE A POPULAR ADDITION TO THE SERIES AND WAS GIVEN HIS OWN SOLO STORIES IN THE PAGES OF ***STAR-SPANGLED COMICS***, STARTING WITH ISSUE #65 (FEBRUARY 1947). THE FIRST STORY, ***"THE TEEN-AGE TERRORS,"*** PLAYED INTO THE YOUTHFULNESS OF THE CHARACTER.

THE INSPIRATION FOR ROBIN'S CREATORS CAME NOT FROM THE RED-BREASTED BIRD BUT FROM ***ROBIN HOOD***. JERRY ROBINSON ATTRIBUTED ARTIST N.C. WYETH'S ROBIN HOOD ILLUSTRATIONS WITH GUIDING THE ***LOOK*** AND ***FEEL*** OF THE CHARACTER.

THIS ISSUE OF ***DETECTIVE COMICS*** ALSO FEATURED AN ADVENTURE STARRING ***SLAM BRADLEY***, A TOUGH-AS-NAILS, HARDBOILED PRIVATE DETECTIVE, CREATED BY JERRY SIEGEL AND JOE SHUSTER, THE CREATORS OF ***SUPERMAN***.

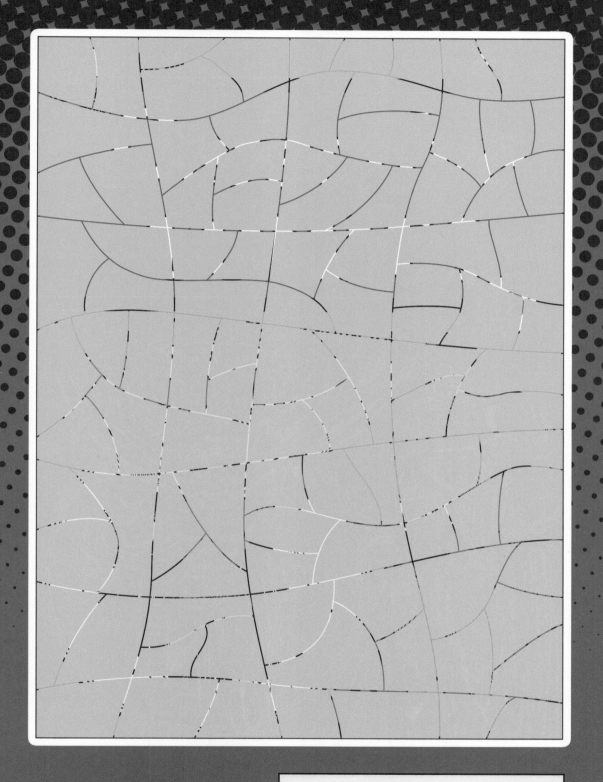

DETECTIVE COMICS #38
APRIL 1940
ART BY BOB KANE, JERRY ROBINSON

GREEN LANTERN™

"THREE TIMES SHALL I FLAME GREEN!"

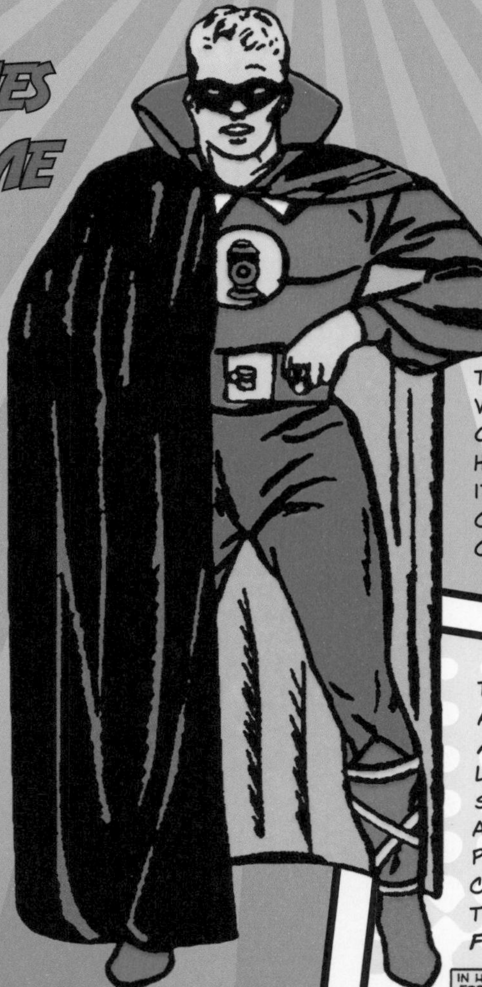

CAME THE EERIE VOICE FROM THE STRANGE, GREEN METEOR. "FIRST, TO BRING ***DEATH***! SECOND, TO BRING ***LIFE***! THIRD, TO BRING ***POWER***!"

THE STORY OF THE ORIGINAL GREEN LANTERN BEGAN MORE THAN ***TWO THOUSAND YEARS AGO*** WHEN THE METEOR ***SLICED THROUGH THE EARTH'S ATMOSPHERE*** AND LANDED SOMEWHERE IN CHINA. A MAN NAMED CHANG DISCOVERED THE METEOR AND USED PART OF IT TO POWER AN ***EMERALD LANTERN***. CHANG WAS THEN KILLED BY A MOB WHO WAS AFRAID OF THE GREEN, GLOWING LANTERN.

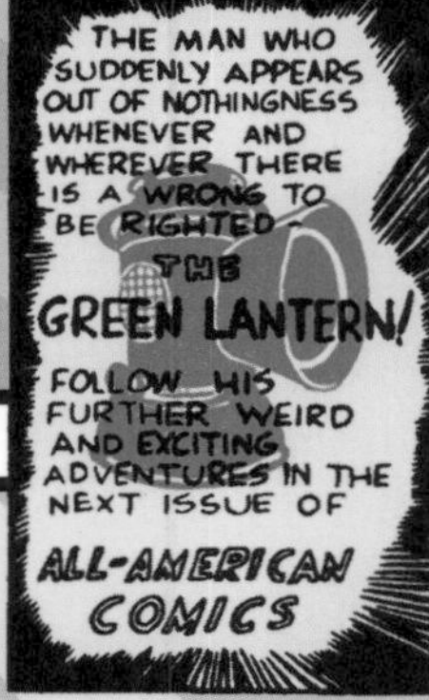
THE MAN WHO SUDDENLY APPEARS OUT OF NOTHINGNESS WHENEVER AND WHEREVER THERE IS A WRONG TO BE RIGHTED — THE GREEN LANTERN! FOLLOW HIS FURTHER WEIRD AND EXCITING ADVENTURES IN THE NEXT ISSUE OF ALL-AMERICAN COMICS

CENTURIES LATER, THE LANTERN EVENTUALLY WOUND UP IN THE HANDS OF A MAN NAMED BILLINGS. HE REWORKED THE LANTERN SO IT RESEMBLED THAT OF A TRAIN CONDUCTOR'S. ***THE GREEN FLAME*** CURED HIM OF AN ILLNESS AND ***RESTORED HIS LIFE***.

THE LANTERN HAD ALREADY BESTOWED ***DEATH AND LIFE***. THAT LEFT ONLY POWER. THE LANTERN GAVE THAT TO ***ALAN SCOTT***, THE SOLE SURVIVOR OF A TRAIN DERAILED BY AN ACT OF SABOTAGE. FASHIONING A SMALL PIECE OF THE LANTERN INTO A RING, SCOTT CATCHES THE MAN RESPONSIBLE FOR THE TERRIBLE ACCIDENT AND BECOMES ***THE FIRST GREEN LANTERN***.

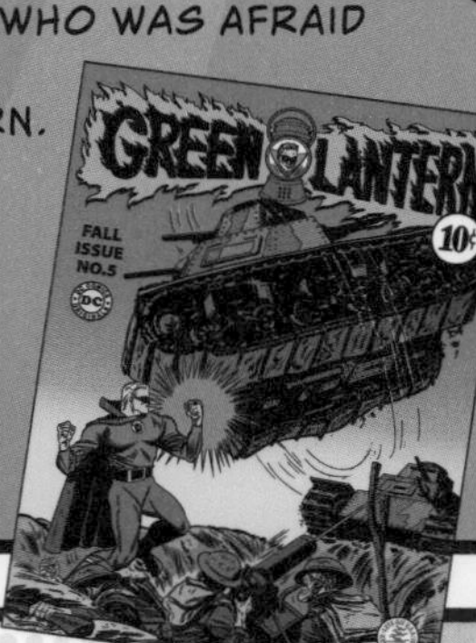
GREEN LANTERN
FALL ISSUE NO.5
10¢

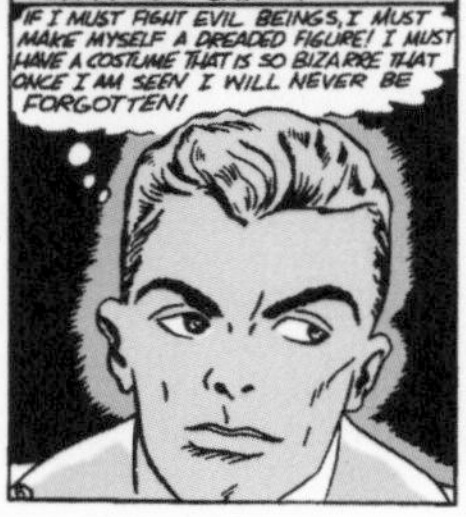
IN HIS SANCTUM, ALAN PREPARES FOR A NEW CAREER.
IF I MUST FIGHT EVIL BEINGS, I MUST MAKE MYSELF A DREADED FIGURE! I MUST HAVE A COSTUME THAT IS SO BIZARRE THAT ONCE I AM SEEN I WILL NEVER BE FORGOTTEN!

NOT ONLY DID ***ALL-AMERICAN COMICS #16*** INTRODUCE GREEN LANTERN TO THE WORLD, BUT IT ALSO SHOWCASED THE AMAZING ARTWORK OF LEGENDARY ARTISTS SHELDON MOLDOFF ON THE COVER AND MARTIN NODELL ON THE INTERIORS.

CREATED BY ***MARTIN NODELL***, THE FIRST GREEN LANTERN FACED STANDARD ***CRIMINALS AND THUGS*** FOR MUCH OF HIS EARLIER CAREER. BUT HE ALSO FOUGHT THE SEEMINGLY IMMORTAL ***VANDAL SAVAGE*** AND THE ZOMBIFIED MENACE OF ***SOLOMON GRUNDY***.

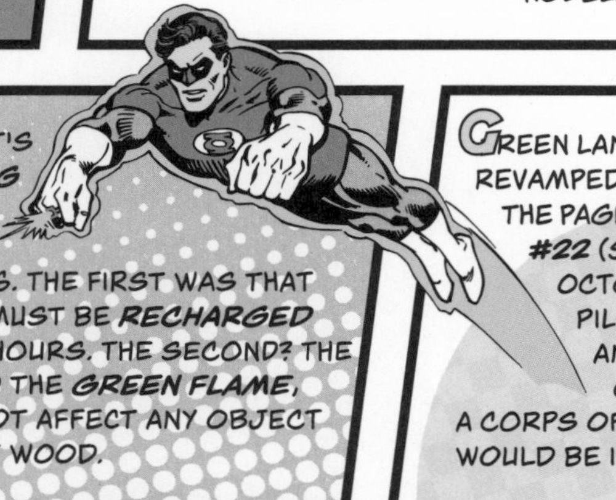

ALAN SCOTT'S ***POWER RING*** HAD TWO NOTABLE LIMITATIONS. THE FIRST WAS THAT THE RING MUST BE ***RECHARGED*** EVERY 24 HOURS. THE SECOND? THE RING, AND THE ***GREEN FLAME***, COULD NOT AFFECT ANY OBJECT MADE OF WOOD.

GREEN LANTERN WOULD BE REVAMPED AND REVISED IN THE PAGES OF ***SHOWCASE #22*** (SEPTEMBER-OCTOBER 1959) AS TEST PILOT ***HAL JORDAN***, AND THE CONCEPT OF GREEN LANTERNS AS A CORPS OF "***SPACE POLICE***" WOULD BE INTRODUCED.

GREEN LANTERN / STICKERS ON PAGE 61. SOLUTION ON PAGE 41.

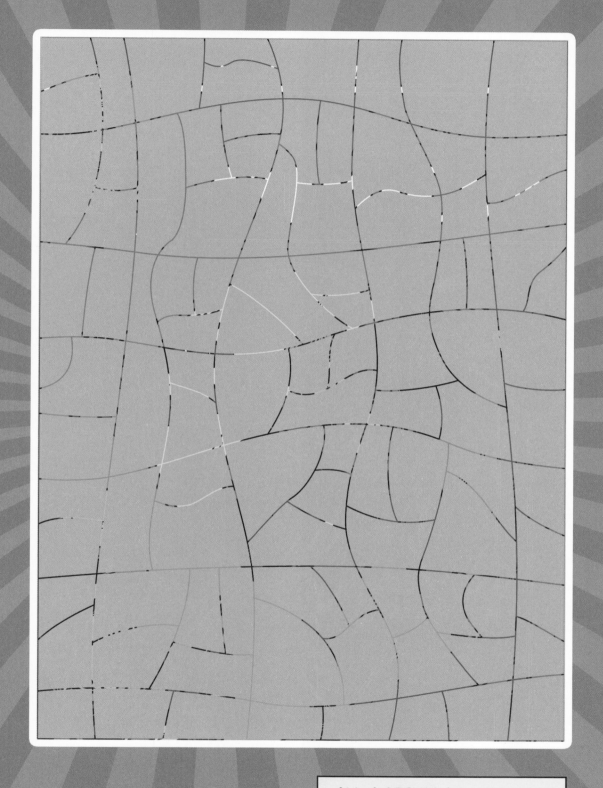

ALL-AMERICAN COMICS #16
JULY 1940
ART BY SHELDON MOLDOFF

THE JOKER

PERHAPS THE QUINTESSENTIAL VILLAIN

OF ALL TIME, ***THE JOKER*** LOOMS LEGENDARY OVER THE LEGACY OF BATMAN. KNOWN AS THE CLOWN PRINCE OF CRIME, THE JOKER IS A BRASH, UNPREDICTABLE, SINISTER FORCE OF ***CHAOTIC EVIL***.

TO SAY THAT THE JOKER WASN'T AN ORDINARY CRIMINAL WAS AN ***UNDERSTATEMENT***. UNLIKE OTHER LAWBREAKERS OF THE TIME, THE JOKER WASN'T IN IT FOR MONETARY GAIN. HE MARCHED TO THE BEAT OF HIS OWN EERIE, INTERNAL DRUM AND WASN'T ABOVE KILLING TO GET WHAT HE WANTED. HIS METHODS WERE GRUESOME, AS IN THE CASE OF HIS PATENTED ***"JOKER VENOM,"*** A POISON THAT WOULD KILL ITS INTENDED TARGET AND LEAVE A ***HORRIFYING GRIN*** ON THEIR FACES.

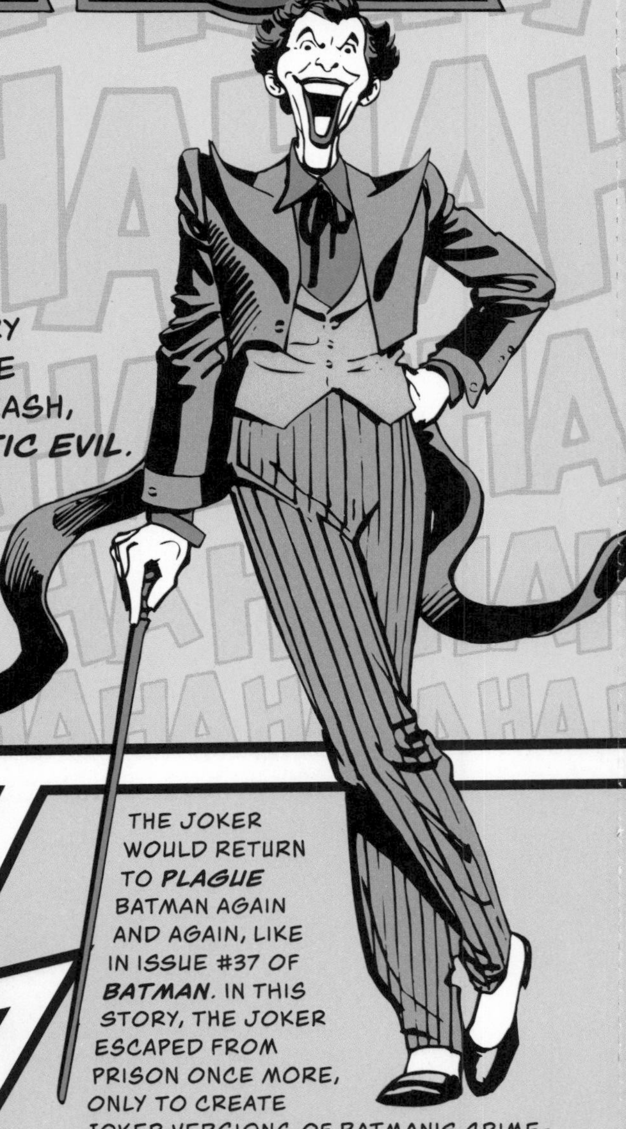

FROM HIS ***FIRST APPEARANCE***, THE JOKER PROVED MOST DEVIOUS. CAPTURED BY BATMAN AND ROBIN FOLLOWING AN UNSUCCESSFUL ROBBERY, THE ***MASTER OF MAYHEM AND MIRTH*** ESCAPED FROM PRISON THANKS TO EXPLOSIVE CHEMICALS HIDDEN INSIDE FALSE TEETH. HE EMBARKS ON A SERIES OF CRIMES UNTIL HE'S MORTALLY WOUNDED IN COMBAT WITH BATMAN.

OR SO WE THINK.

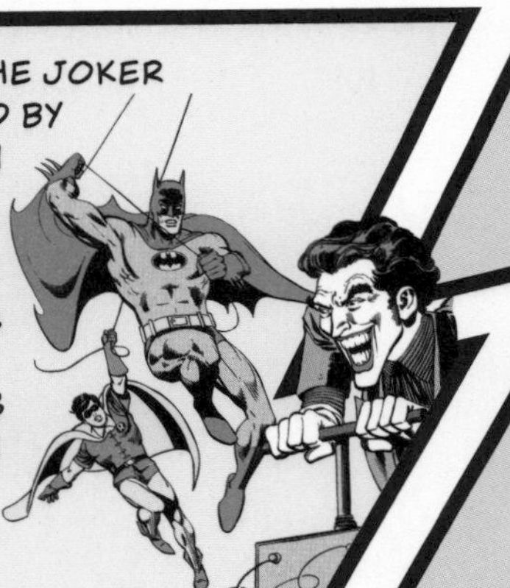

THE JOKER WOULD RETURN TO ***PLAGUE*** BATMAN AGAIN AND AGAIN, LIKE IN ISSUE #37 OF ***BATMAN***. IN THIS STORY, THE JOKER ESCAPED FROM PRISON ONCE MORE, ONLY TO CREATE JOKER VERSIONS OF BATMAN'S CRIME-FIGHTING TOOLS: THE JOKER-SIGNAL, THE JOKERMOBILE, AND THE JOKER-GYRO.

THE JOKER MADE HIS FIRST APPEARANCE IN ***BATMAN #1*** (MARCH 1940). THE CLOWN CHARACTER WAS SLATED FOR TWO STORIES AND THEN WAS SUPPOSED TO DIE--FOR GOOD!--AT THE END OF THE SECOND. HOWEVER, EDITOR WHITNEY ELLSWORTH WANTED TO KEEP THE JOKER AS AN ONGOING VILLAIN FOR THE DARK KNIGHT.

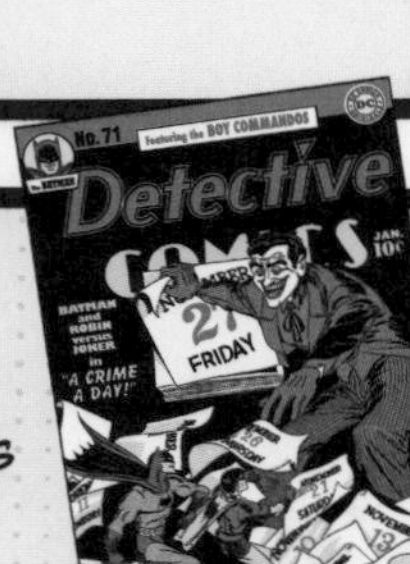
No. 71
Detective
27
FRIDAY

ONE OF THE MOST ICONIC COVERS TO FEATURE THE JOKER WAS ***DETECTIVE COMICS #71*** (JANUARY 1943), DEPICTING THE CLOWN PRINCE OF CRIME TEARING PAGES FROM A CALENDAR AND HURLING THEM AT A BELEAGUERED BATMAN AND ROBIN!

IN THE 1966 LIVE-ACTION *BATMAN* TV SERIES, ACTOR ***CESAR ROMERO*** REFUSED TO SHAVE HIS MUSTACHE FOR THE ROLE OF ***THE JOKER***, SO THE MAKEUP TEAM POWDERED RIGHT OVER IT TO MATCH THE JOKER'S CLOWN-WHITE SKIN!

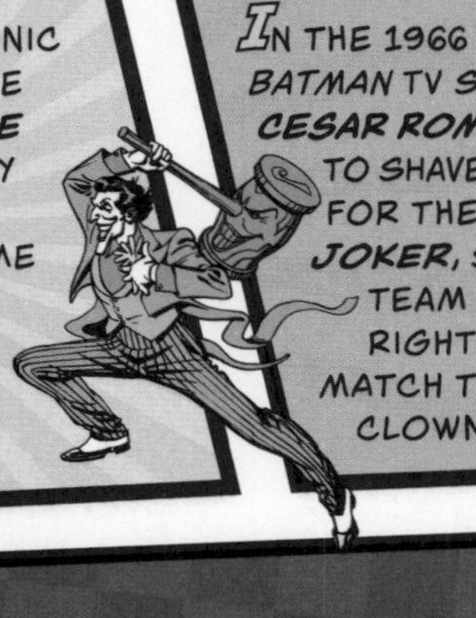

THE JOKER / STICKERS ON PAGE 64. SOLUTION ON PAGE 42.

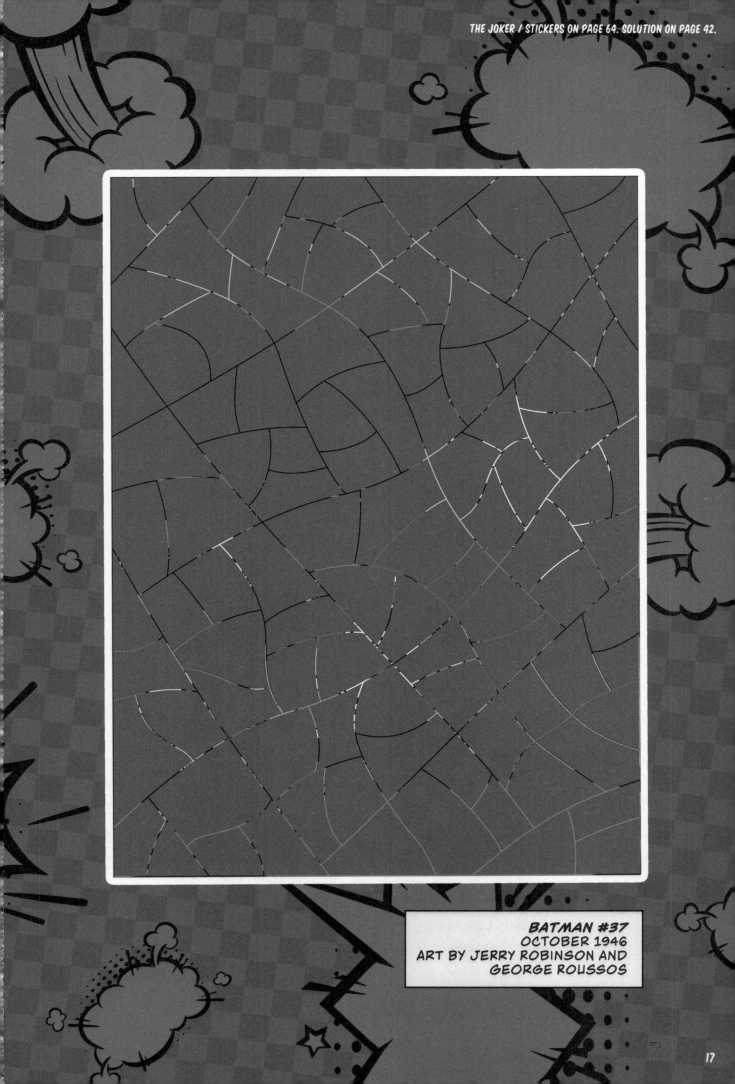

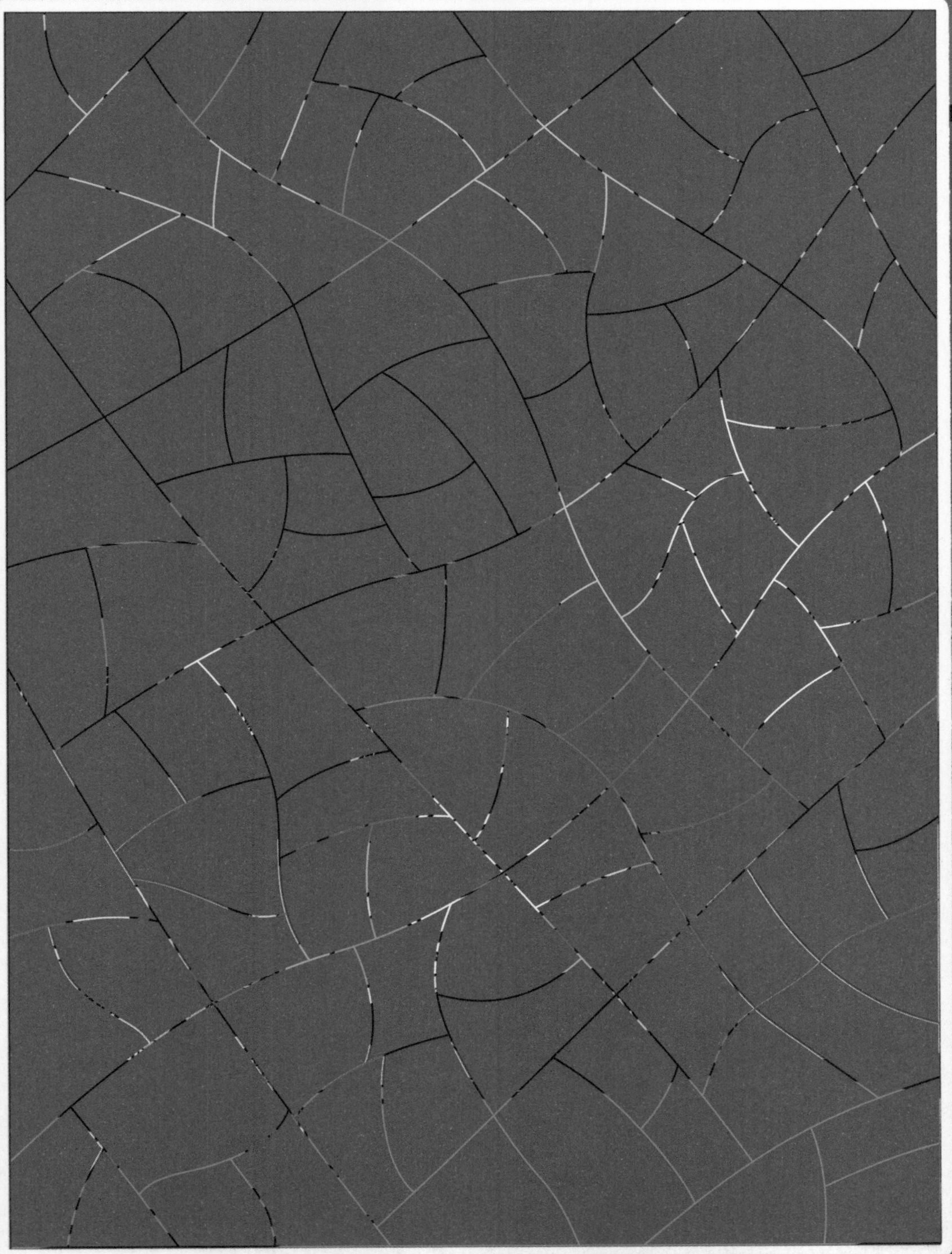

BATMAN #37
OCTOBER 1946
ART BY JERRY ROBINSON AND
GEORGE ROUSSOS

THE Riddler

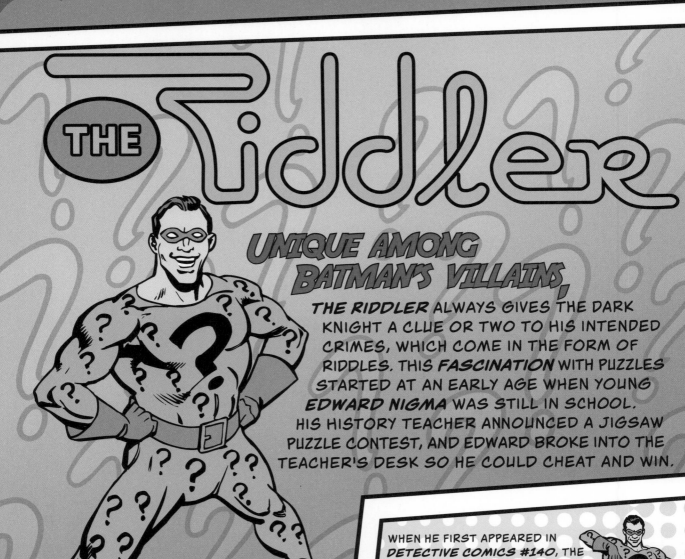

UNIQUE AMONG BATMAN'S VILLAINS,

THE RIDDLER ALWAYS GIVES THE DARK KNIGHT A CLUE OR TWO TO HIS INTENDED CRIMES, WHICH COME IN THE FORM OF RIDDLES. THIS *FASCINATION* WITH PUZZLES STARTED AT AN EARLY AGE WHEN YOUNG *EDWARD NIGMA* WAS STILL IN SCHOOL. HIS HISTORY TEACHER ANNOUNCED A JIGSAW PUZZLE CONTEST, AND EDWARD BROKE INTO THE TEACHER'S DESK SO HE COULD CHEAT AND WIN.

FROM THAT DAY ON, EDWARD WOULD BECOME *OBSESSED* WITH PUZZLES, ESPECIALLY RIDDLES. ALWAYS WANTING TO PROVE HIMSELF, HE WOULD CHALLENGE THE POLICE AND, EVENTUALLY, *BATMAN HIMSELF*. EDWARD—WHO THEN ASSUMED THE MASKED IDENTITY OF THE RIDDLER, COMPLETE WITH A COLORFUL QUESTION-MARK-THEMED OUTFIT—WASN'T INTRIGUED BY CRIMINAL ACTIVITY. HE WAS MORE INTERESTED IN *SOLVING PUZZLES.*

WHEN HE FIRST APPEARED IN *DETECTIVE COMICS #140*, THE RIDDLER BAFFLED BATMAN AND ROBIN WITH AN ENORMOUS ELECTRIC CROSSWORD PUZZLE THAT FEATURED THE CLUE "BASIN STREET BANQUET." THE DYNAMIC DUO BELIEVED THIS TO BE A REFERENCE TO THE GOTHAM CITY MAYOR'S CHARITY DINNER, BUT IT WAS ACTUALLY ABOUT A BANK THE RIDDLER HAD FLOODED— "BANQUET" MEANING "BANK WET."

THEIR *BATTLE OF WITS* TOOK THEM TO THE PLEASURE PIER AMUSEMENT PARK WHERE THE RIDDLER SUPPOSEDLY MET HIS DEMISE WHEN THE PIER EXPLODED. AS WITH MOST VILLAINS, THIS WAS HARDLY THE END FOR THE RIDDLER. RATHER, IT WAS *ONLY THE BEGINNING.*

*B*EFORE HE BECAME *THE RIDDLER*, EDWARD NIGMA WORKED IN A CARNIVAL WHERE HE WOULD CHEAT PATRONS OUT OF THEIR MONEY BY *FIXING GAMES*. HE SOON GREW BORED WITH FLEECING CUSTOMERS AND SET HIS SIGHTS ON *BATMAN AND ROBIN*.

*T*HE RIDDLER WOULD SOON RETURN IN ISSUE #142 OF *DETECTIVE COMICS* (DECEMBER 1948) WHERE HE CREATES A PUZZLE CONTEST THAT DRIVES THE CITIZENS OF GOTHAM CITY WILD.

*S*EVERAL ACTORS HAVE PORTRAYED THE RIDDLING CHARACTER IN VARIOUS TV AND FILM PROJECTS, NOTABLY FRANK GORSHIN, JOHN ASTIN, JIM CARREY, AND CORY MICHAEL SMITH.

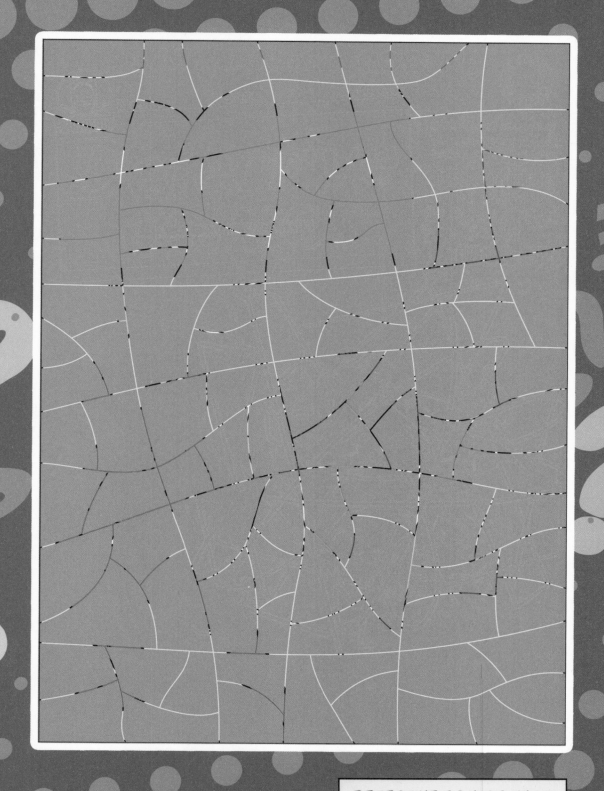

DETECTIVE COMICS #140
OCTOBER 1948
ART BY WIN MORTIMER

CATWOMAN

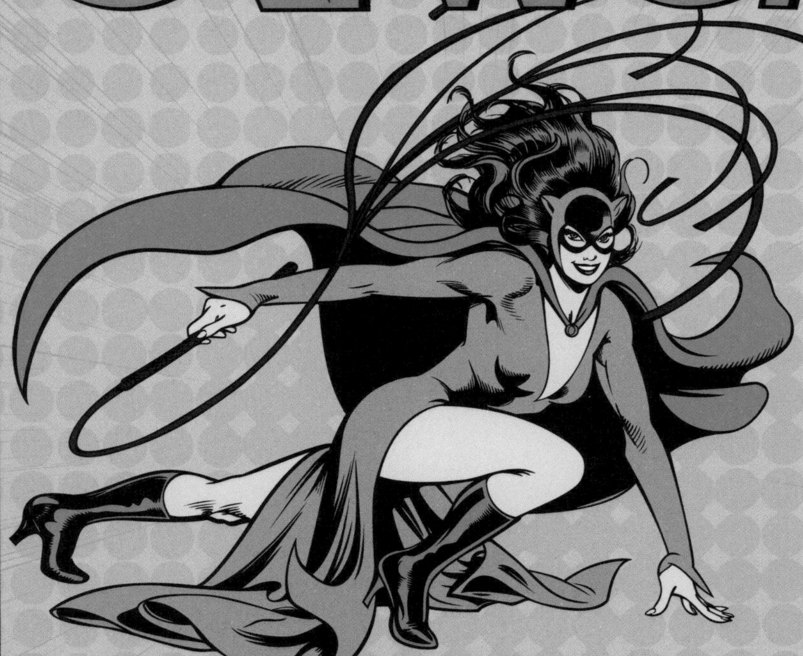

SELINA KYLE

EMERGED EARLY IN BATMAN'S CAREER TO ***BEDEVIL*** THE WORLD'S GREATEST DETECTIVE. BUT SHE WASN'T ALWAYS CALLED ***CATWOMAN.*** IN HER FIRST APPEARANCE, SHE WAS REFERRED TO SIMPLY AS "THE CAT." APPROPRIATELY ENOUGH, SHE WAS A ***CAT BURGLAR*** AND ***JEWEL THIEF***, THOUGH SHE DID NOT WEAR HER ICONIC CAT OUTFIT DURING HER FIRST CONFRONTATION WITH BATMAN.

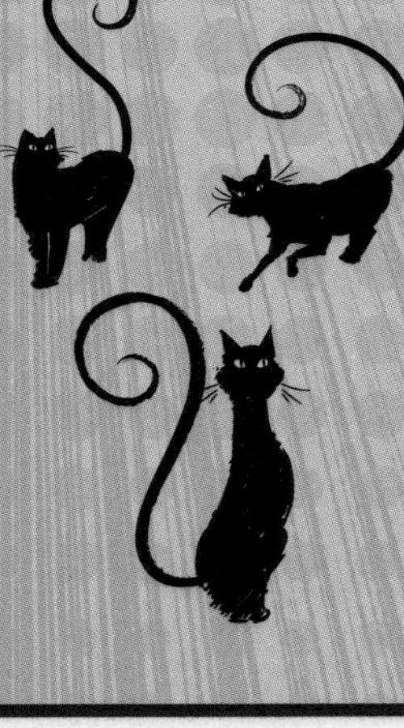

IT WASN'T UNTIL THEIR THIRD MEETING THAT "THE CAT" WOULD APPEAR WEARING A FURRY CAT MASK, HER ***TRUE IDENTITY*** DISGUISED FROM PRYING EYES. NOW KNOWN AS "***CAT-WOMAN,***" SHE SUCCEEDS IN ELUDING JUSTICE BY DISTRACTING BATMAN WITH A KISS, EFFECTING HER ESCAPE.

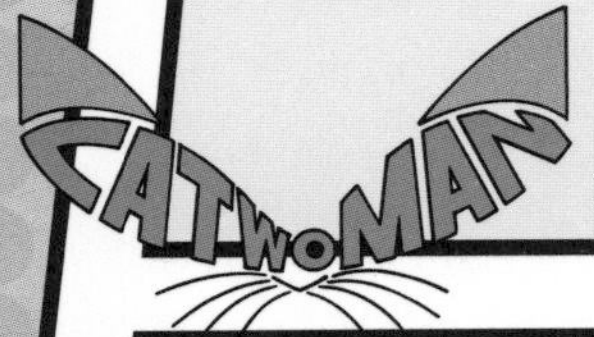
CATWOMAN

WHEN BATMAN AND ROBIN ENCOUNTER SELINA IN "CATWOMAN--EMPRESS OF THE UNDERWORLD," SHE HAS APPARENTLY ***GONE STRAIGHT*** AND IS NOW RUNNING A PET SHOP IN GOTHAM CITY. A WAVE OF CAT-RELATED CRIMES SEEMS TO POINT HER WAY, YET SHE MAINTAINS HER INNOCENCE. THE CRIMES ARE REVEALED TO BE THE WORK OF WHALE MORTON AND HIS GANG WHO COERCE CATWOMAN TO ***RETURN TO CRIME.***

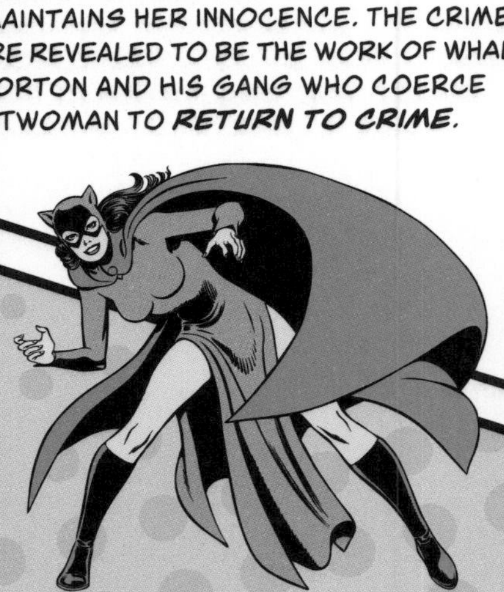

BATMAN AND ROBIN TRACK DOWN THE CRIMINALS BUT ARE CAPTURED. ***THE DARK KNIGHT*** MANAGES TO ESCAPE AND IS SURPRISED TO FIND CATWOMAN HELPING HIM DEFEAT WHALE MORTON'S GANG. IT'S REVEALED THAT CATWOMAN HAD BEEN A ***DOUBLE AGENT***, WORKING FROM WITHIN TO STOP THE GANG THE WHOLE TIME!

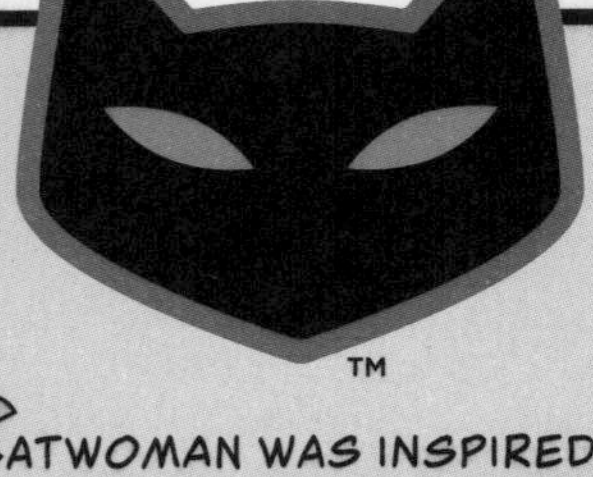

TM

CATWOMAN WAS INSPIRED IN PART BY THE ON-SCREEN PERSONA OF 1930S ACTRESS ***JEAN HARLOW.***

ISSUE #65 OF ***BATMAN*** SAW CATWOMAN TURNING OVER A NEW LEAF BY TRYING TO ***WALK A RIGHTEOUS PATH.*** SHE CONTINUED TO HELP BATMAN OVER THE NEXT COUPLE OF YEARS BUT EVENTUALLY RETURNED TO A ***LIFE OF CRIME*** IN ***DETECTIVE COMICS #203.***

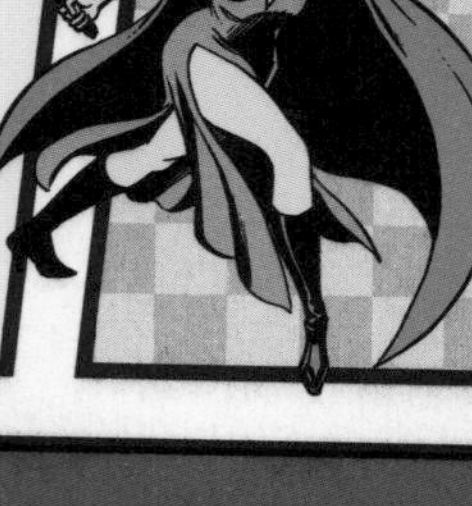

CATWOMAN WOULD BECOME AN ***INTEGRAL PART*** OF BATMAN'S EARLY YEARS IN THE FRANK MILLER/ DAVID MAZZUCCHELLI OPUS ***BATMAN: YEAR ONE,*** ORIGINALLY APPEARING IN ***BATMAN #404-407*** (FEBRUARY-MAY 1987).

CATWOMAN / STICKERS ON PAGE 68. SOLUTION ON PAGE 44.

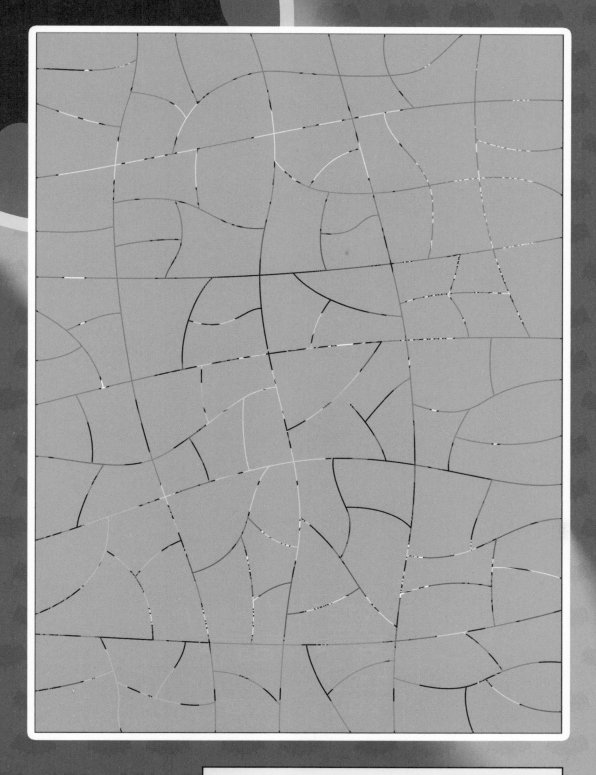

BATMAN #65
JULY 1951
ART BY WIN MORTIMER, LEW SAYRE SCHWARTZ,
CHARLES PARIS, IRA SCHNAPP

THE FLASH

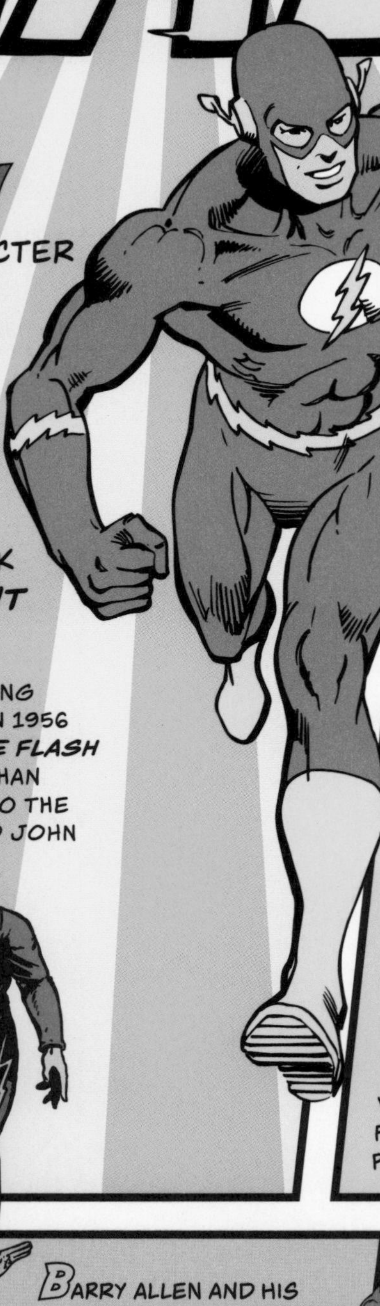

THE FIRST FLASH

WAS JAY GARRICK, A CHARACTER WHO APPEARED IN COMICS' GOLDEN AGE, IN THE PAGES OF *FLASH COMICS #1* (JANUARY 1940). POSSESSED OF *SUPER-SPEED* DERIVED FROM INHALING THE VAPORS FROM HARD WATER, GARRICK USED HIS ABILITIES TO *FIGHT CRIME*.

THE CHARACTER PROVED POPULAR AMONG READERS, AND WHEN THE TIME CAME IN 1956 TO REVIVE SOME OF DC'S HEROES, *THE FLASH* WAS FIRST ON THE LIST. BUT RATHER THAN SIMPLY BRINGING JAY GARRICK BACK TO THE FOLD, WRITERS ROBERT KANIGHER AND JOHN BROOME TEAMED WITH ARTIST CARMINE INFANTINO TO DELIVER SOMETHING *ENTIRELY DIFFERENT.*

THIS NEW, UPDATED FLASH WAS *BARRY ALLEN*, A POLICE SCIENTIST WHO GAINED THE POWER OF SUPER-SPEED THANKS TO A CHEMICAL BATH CAUSED BY AN *ERRANT LIGHTNING BOLT.* IT WAS REVEALED THAT ALLEN WAS IN FACT A FAN OF THE ORIGINAL FLASH HIMSELF, HAVING READ THAT CHARACTER'S COMICS. TAKING THAT NAME, ALLEN BECAME THE SECOND SUPER HERO TO BE CALLED *THE FLASH.*

IN HIS FIRST APPEARANCE IN *SHOWCASE #4*, BARRY NOT ONLY ACQUIRED HIS *AMAZING NEW POWERS*, BUT HE ALSO FACED HIS FIRST FOE--THE WORLD'S SLOWEST PERSON, NAMED, APPROPRIATELY ENOUGH, TURTLE MAN. THE FLASH THEN WENT UP AGAINST MAZDAN, A CRIMINAL FROM THE FUTURE SENT TO THE FLASH'S PRESENT BY MISTAKE.

THE FLASH KEPT HIS COSTUME HIDDEN INSIDE A *RING* THAT HE ALWAYS WORE. THE COSTUME WOULD *EXPAND UPON CONTACT* WITH THE AIR, ALLOWING BARRY ALLEN TO ALWAYS HAVE HIS UNIFORM HANDY.

BARRY ALLEN AND HIS PRECURSOR, *JAY GARRICK*, WOULD MEET IN *THE FLASH #123*, IN A STORY ENTITLED *"FLASH OF TWO WORLDS"* BY WRITER GARDNER FOX AND ARTIST CARMINE INFANTINO. IT MARKED THE FIRST TIME A GOLDEN-AGE DC CHARACTER MET THEIR SILVER-AGE COUNTERPART.

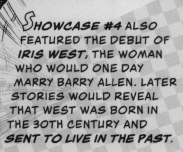

SHOWCASE #4 ALSO FEATURED THE DEBUT OF *IRIS WEST*, THE WOMAN WHO WOULD ONE DAY MARRY BARRY ALLEN. LATER STORIES WOULD REVEAL THAT WEST WAS BORN IN THE 30TH CENTURY AND *SENT TO LIVE IN THE PAST.*

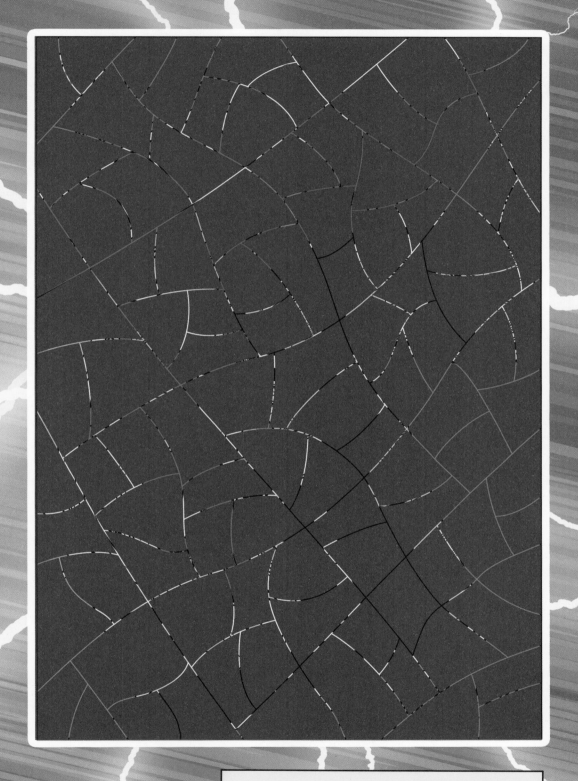

SHOWCASE #4
OCTOBER 1956
ART BY CARMINE INFANTINO, JOE KUBERT

BATWOMAN

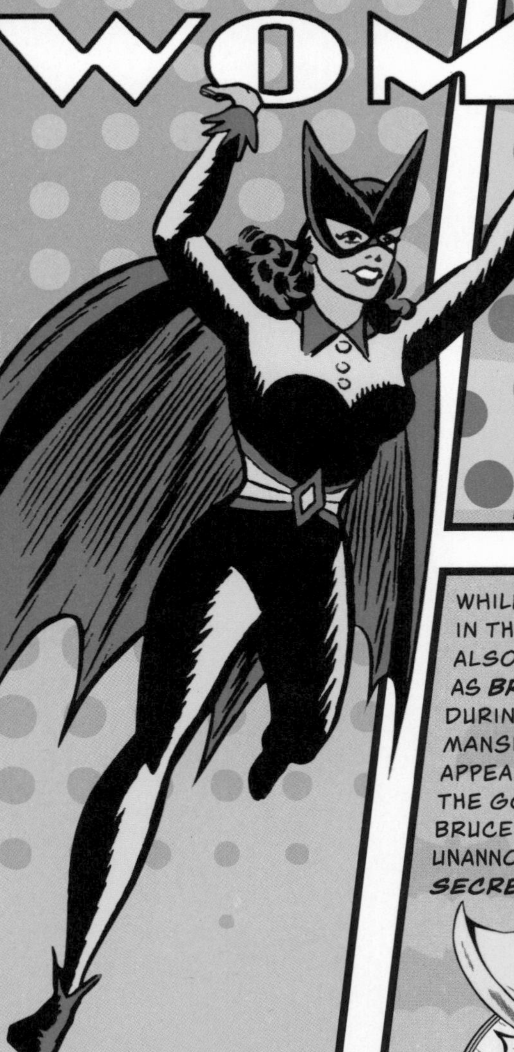

INTRODUCED IN THE PAGES

OF ***DETECTIVE COMICS #233*** (JULY 1956), KATHY KANE WAS A ***WEALTHY GOTHAM CITY HEIRESS***, AS WELL AS A ***CIRCUS AERIALIST.*** SHE DECIDED TO PUT HER SKILLS AND RESOURCES TO USE IN THE COSTUMED DISGUISE OF ***BATWOMAN***, INSPIRED BY THE NOCTURNAL CRIME-FIGHTING ACTIVITIES OF ***THE DARK KNIGHT***.

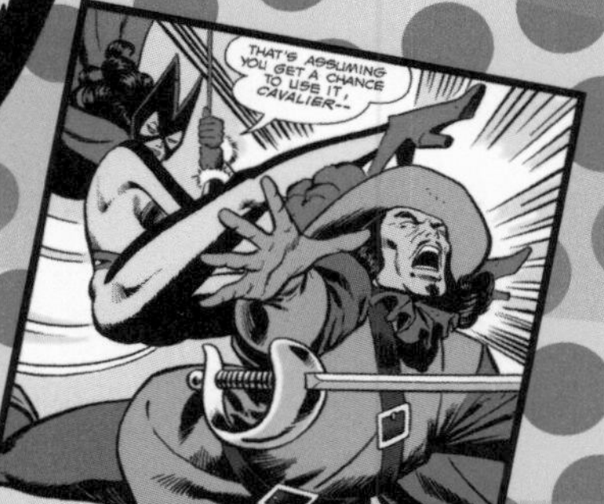
THAT'S ASSUMING YOU GET A CHANCE TO USE IT, CAVALIER--

WHILE THE TWO BECAME INVOLVED IN THEIR SUPER HERO GUISES, THEY ALSO ENCOUNTERED ONE ANOTHER AS ***BRUCE WAYNE*** AND ***KATHY KANE*** DURING A PARTY HELD AT KANE'S MANSION. WHEN THE BAT-SIGNAL APPEARS IN THE SKY HIGH ABOVE THE GOTHAM CITY SKYLINE, BOTH BRUCE AND KATHY LEAVE THE PARTY UNANNOUNCED TO CHANGE INTO THEIR ***SECRET IDENTITIES.***

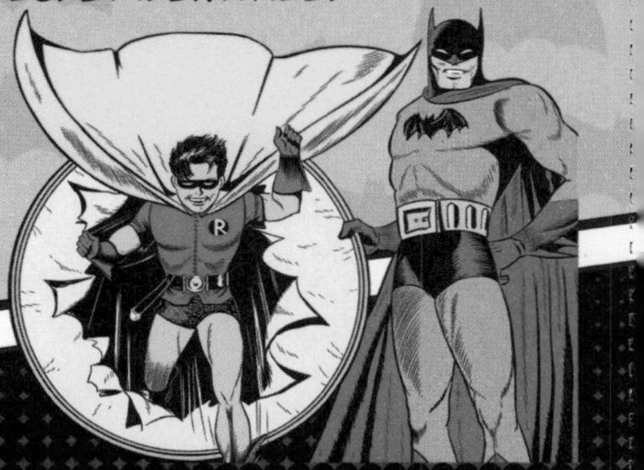

BATWOMAN WAS A ***SUCCESSFUL CRIME FIGHTER***, USING HER CIRCUS-HONED ABILITIES AND CLEVER GADGETRY IN HER ***FIGHT AGAINST EVIL.*** THIS ATTRACTED THE ATTENTION OF BATMAN, WHO BELIEVED BATWOMAN'S LUCK WOULD SOON RUN OUT AND SHE MIGHT FALL VICTIM TO THE VERY CRIMINALS SHE TRIED TO APPREHEND.

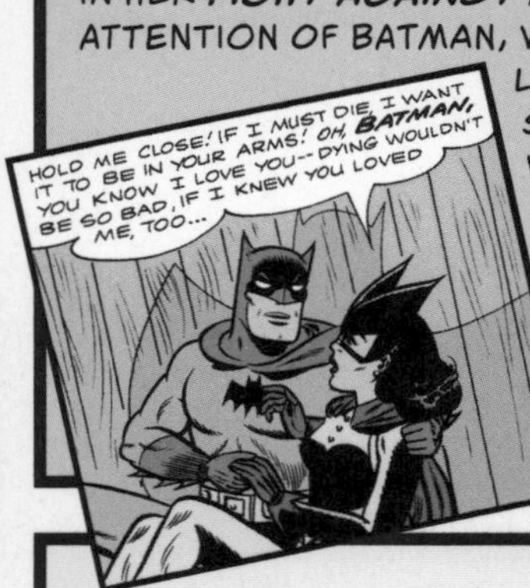
HOLD ME CLOSE! IF I MUST DIE, I WANT IT TO BE IN YOUR ARMS! OH, BATMAN, YOU KNOW I LOVE YOU-- DYING WOULDN'T BE SO BAD, IF I KNEW YOU LOVED ME, TOO...

ULTIMATELY, ***BATWOMAN*** AND ***BATMAN*** WORK TOGETHER TO CATCH HUGO VORN AND HIS CRIMINAL GANG. BATMAN DISCOVERS THAT KANE IS SECRETLY BATWOMAN, BUT BEFORE HE CAN CONFRONT HER, BATWOMAN REVEALS THAT SHE KNOWS ***EXACTLY*** WHO BATMAN AND ROBIN ARE!

BATGIRL

BATWOMAN WAS CREATED AS PART OF AN ONGOING EFFORT TO EXPAND BATMAN'S SUPPORTING ***CAST OF CHARACTERS.***

BATMAN

IT WOULD BE REVEALED IN ***BATMAN #139*** (APRIL 1961) THAT ***KATHY KANE'S NIECE***, BETTY, HAD TAKEN THE COSTUMED IDENTITY OF ***BAT-GIRL.*** WORKING WITH HER AUNT AND BATMAN AND ROBIN, BAT-GIRL HELPS TO TAKE DOWN KING COBRA AND THE COBRA GANG.

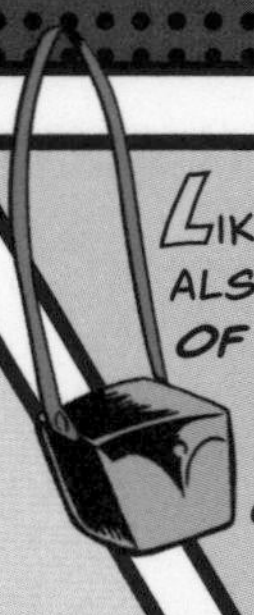

LIKE BATMAN, BATWOMAN ALSO CARRIED AN ***ARRAY OF DEVICES*** TO HELP WITH HER BATTLE AGAINST CRIME. BUT INSTEAD OF A UTILITY BELT, SHE CARRIED HER TOOLS IN A UTILITY BAG ***SLUNG OVER HER SHOULDER.***

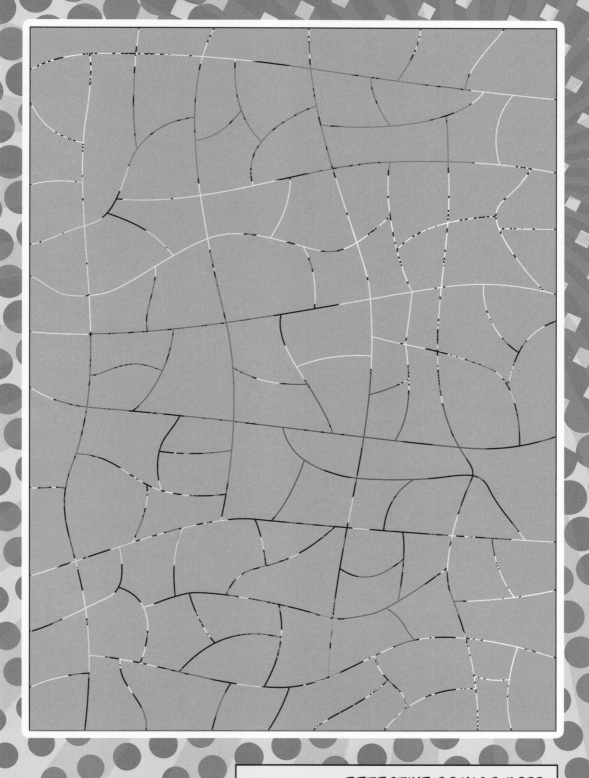

DETECTIVE COMICS #233
JULY 1956
ART BY SHELDON MOLDOFF, IRA SCHNAPP

SUPERGIRL™

IT WAS AN ORDINARY DAY

FOR CLARK KENT UNTIL HIS ***X-RAY VISION*** DETECTED A SLEEK, PURPLE ROCKET PLUMMETING THROUGH EARTH'S ATMOSPHERE AND CRASHING SEVERAL MILES FROM ***THE DAILY PLANET*** IN METROPOLIS. AFTER A QUICK CHANGE INTO HIS ***SECRET IDENTITY*** OF SUPERMAN, HE ARRIVED AT THE CRASH SITE. SUPERMAN WAS STUNNED TO DISCOVER THAT THE ROCKET CONTAINED ONE PERSON: ***A TEENAGE GIRL NAMED KARA.***

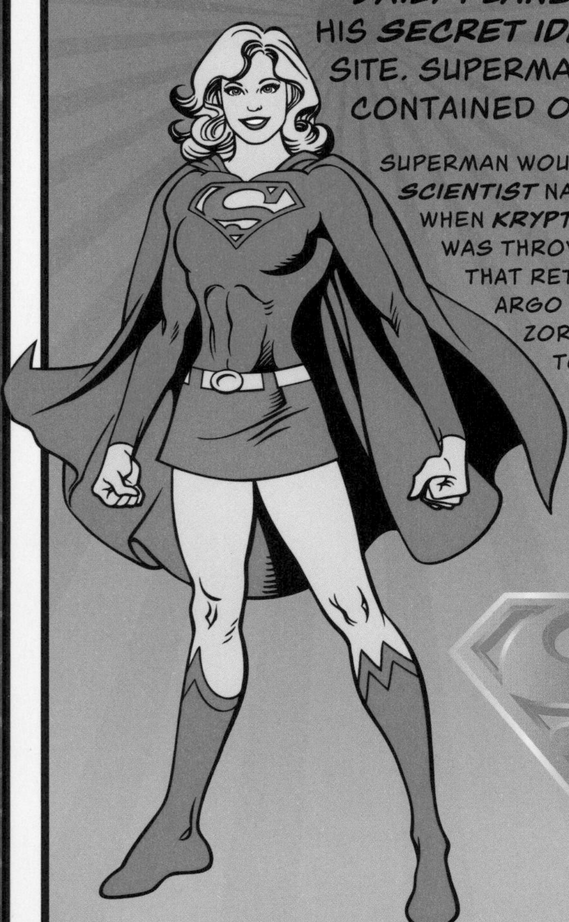

SUPERMAN WOULD SOON LEARN THAT KARA WAS THE DAUGHTER OF A ***KRYPTONIAN SCIENTIST*** NAMED ZOR-EL, THE BROTHER OF SUPERMAN'S OWN FATHER, JOR-EL. WHEN ***KRYPTON EXPLODED***, ARGO CITY--WHERE SHE LIVED WITH HER FATHER--WAS THROWN INTO SPACE INTACT, PROTECTED BY AN ENVIRONMENTAL "BUBBLE" THAT RETAINED THE CITY'S NATURAL ATMOSPHERE. THE GROUND BENEATH ARGO CITY WOULD SOON BECOME ***DEADLY KRYPTONITE***. HOWEVER, ZOR-EL COATED THE GROUND WITH LEAD TO PROTECT THE SURVIVING KRYPTONIANS.

A METEOR SHOWER DAMAGED THE BUBBLE AND LEAD SHIELDING, AND THE INHABITANTS OF ARGO CITY WERE FACED WITH A MOUNTING CRISIS. IN ORDER TO SAVE KARA'S LIFE, ZOR-EL PLACED HER IN THE ROCKET AND SENT HER TO EARTH TO HER COUSIN ***SUPERMAN***.

IN ORDER TO KEEP HIS OWN IDENTITY A SECRET, AND TO PROTECT KARA, SUPERMAN TAKES HIS COUSIN TO THE MIDVALE ORPHANAGE, WHERE SHE ASSUMES THE EARTH IDENTITY OF TEENAGER LINDA LEE. IN SHORT TIME, SHE WOULD JOIN HER COUSIN ON MISSIONS AS ***SUPERGIRL***.

™

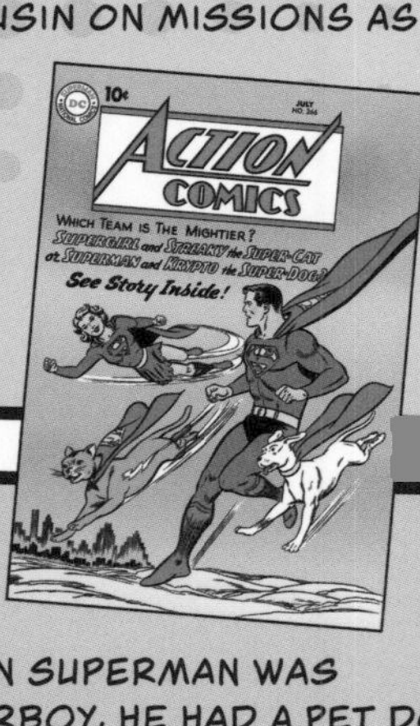
ACTION COMICS
WHICH TEAM IS THE MIGHTIER?
See Story Inside!

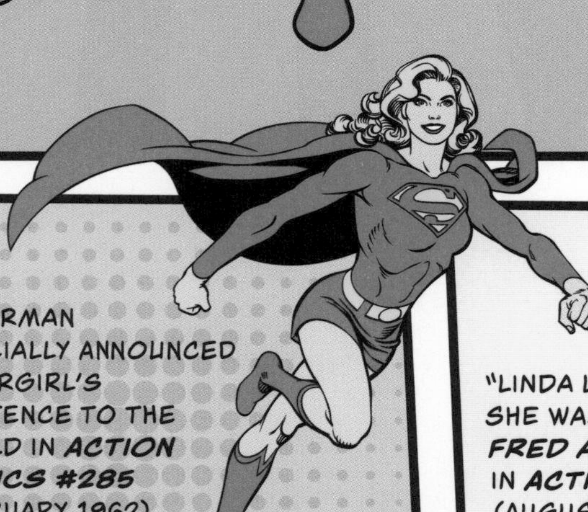

SUPERMAN OFFICIALLY ANNOUNCED SUPERGIRL'S EXISTENCE TO THE WORLD IN ***ACTION COMICS #285*** (FEBRUARY 1962).

KARA WOULD ONLY REMAIN "LINDA LEE" FOR SO LONG. SHE WAS ADOPTED BY ***FRED AND EDNA DANVERS*** IN ***ACTION COMICS #279*** (AUGUST 1961).

WHEN SUPERMAN WAS SUPERBOY, HE HAD A PET DOG NAMED ***KRYPTO THE SUPER-DOG***. SO IT WAS ONLY NATURAL THAT SUPERGIRL WOULD HAVE A PET CAT! ***STREAKY THE SUPER-CAT*** FIRST APPEARED IN ***ACTION COMICS #261*** (FEBRUARY 1960).

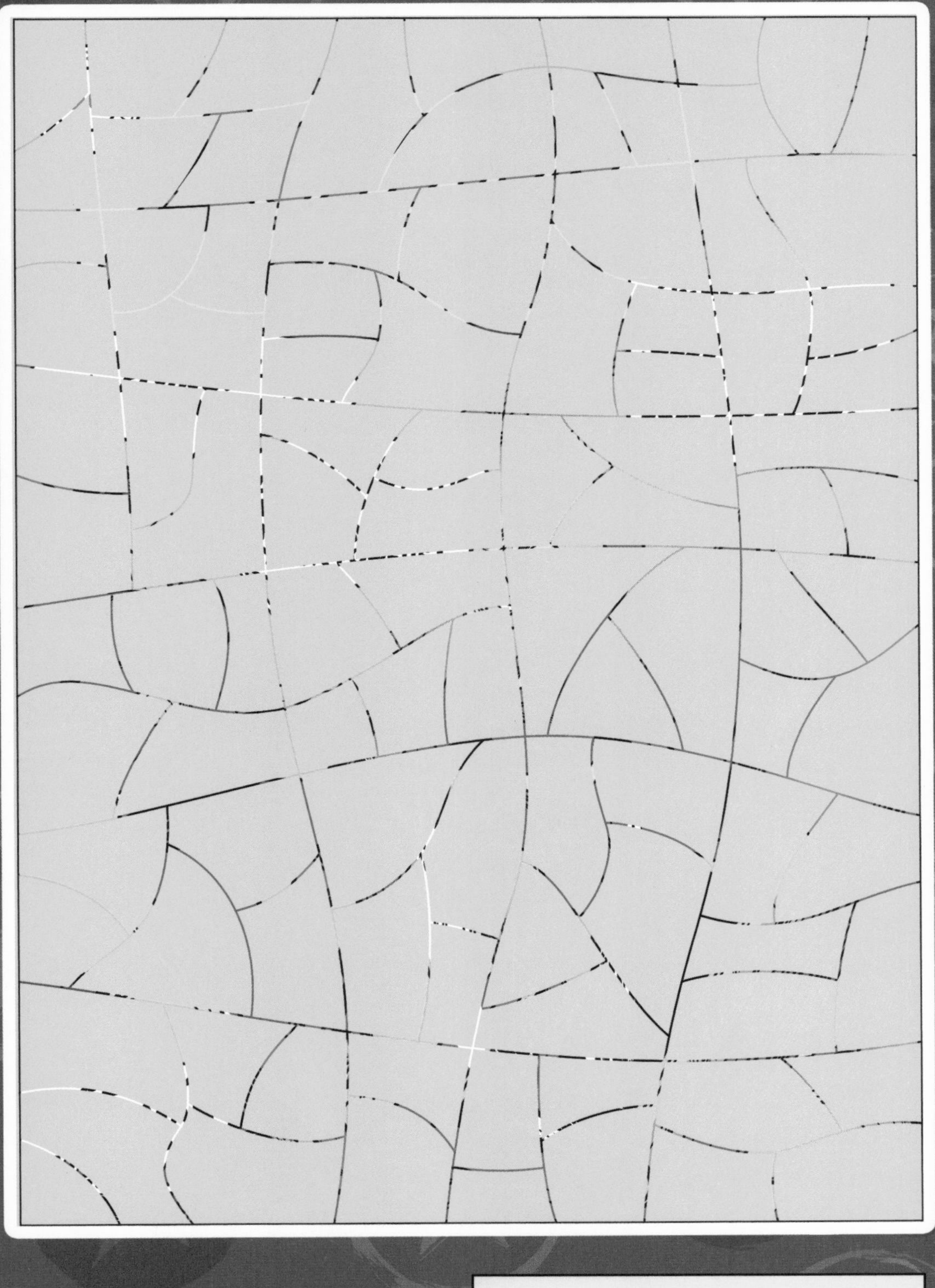

ACTION COMICS #252
MAY 1959
ART BY CURT SWAN, AL PLASTINO

The ATOM

LIKE THE FLASH BEFORE HIM,

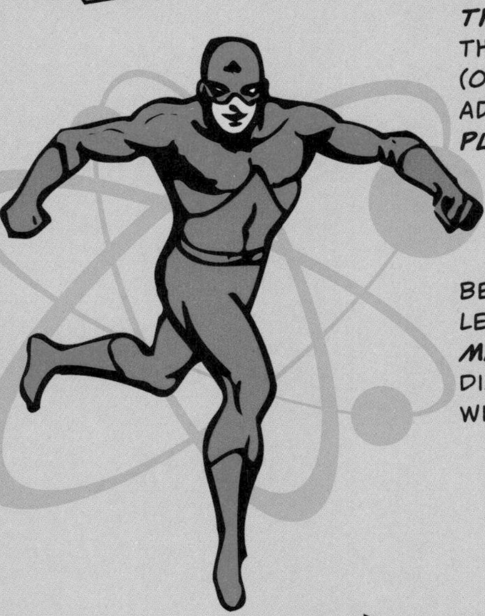

THE ATOM WAS A REVIVAL OF A GOLDEN-AGE SUPER HERO OF THE SAME NAME. INTRODUCED IN ***ALL-AMERICAN COMICS #19*** (OCTOBER 1940), DIMINUTIVE AL PRATT BECAME THE COSTUMED ADVENTURER KNOWN AS THE ATOM. POSSESSED OF AN ***ATOMIC PUNCH***, THE ATOM FOUGHT EVIL ALONGSIDE ***THE JUSTICE SOCIETY***.

BUT IN 1961, THE ATOM WOULD BE BROUGHT BACK IN THE GUISE OF ***PROFESSOR RAY PALMER***, A SCIENTIST WHO STUMBLES UPON A FRAGMENT OF A ***DWARF STAR***. REASONING THAT HE MIGHT BE ABLE TO CONTROL THE SIZE OF OBJECTS, HE CREATES TWO LENSES FROM THE DWARF STAR--IN EFFECT, MAKING A ***SHRINKING MACHINE***. WHILE THE INITIAL TESTS PROVE SUCCESSFUL, PALMER IS DISHEARTENED TO FIND THAT EVERYTHING HE HAS SHRUNK EXPLODES WITHIN AN HOUR.

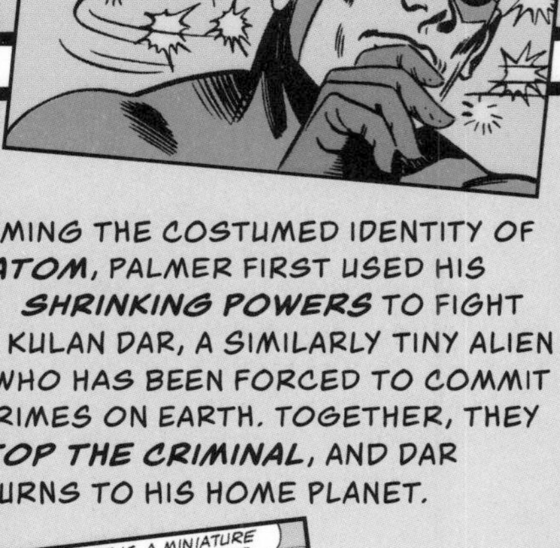
AS HIS FINGER PRESSES DOWN ON THE FIRING PIN--AN INVISIBLE LIGHT BATHES THE WORLD'S SMALLEST SUPER-HERO...
MY NAME IS ... IS...

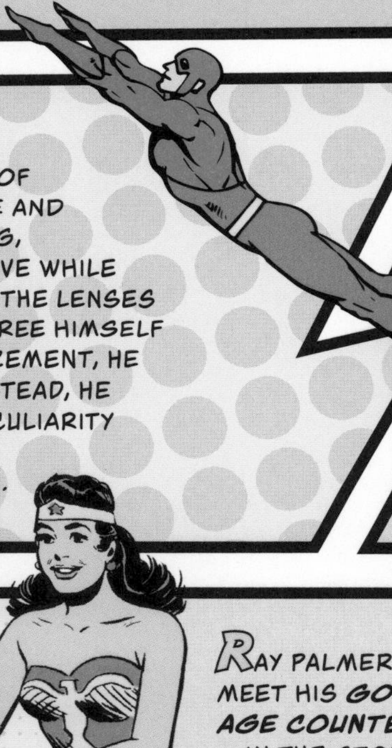

PALMER ONLY USES THE DEVICE ON HIMSELF OUT OF ***DESPERATION***, WHEN HE AND HIS FIANCÉE, JEAN LORING, BECOME TRAPPED IN A CAVE WHILE ON A HIKE. PALMER USES THE LENSES TO ***SHRINK DOWN*** AND FREE HIMSELF AND LORING. TO HIS AMAZEMENT, HE ***DOESN'T EXPLODE***. INSTEAD, HE REALIZES THAT SOME PECULIARITY OF HIS BODY CHEMISTRY ALLOWED HIM TO SURVIVE.

ASSUMING THE COSTUMED IDENTITY OF ***THE ATOM***, PALMER FIRST USED HIS ***SHRINKING POWERS*** TO FIGHT KULAN DAR, A SIMILARLY TINY ALIEN WHO HAS BEEN FORCED TO COMMIT CRIMES ON EARTH. TOGETHER, THEY ***STOP THE CRIMINAL***, AND DAR RETURNS TO HIS HOME PLANET.

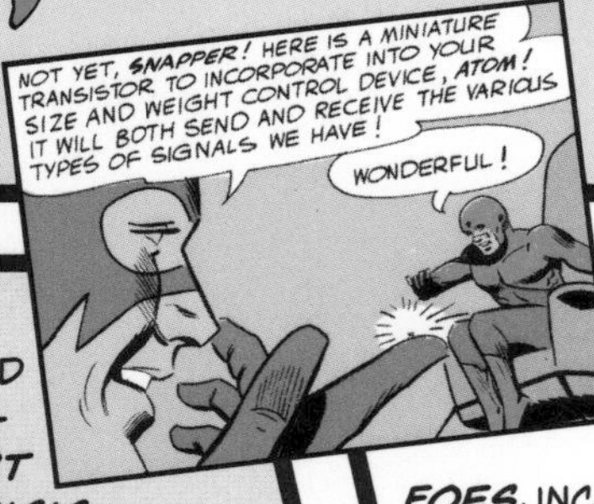
NOT YET, SNAPPER! HERE IS A MINIATURE TRANSISTOR TO INCORPORATE INTO YOUR SIZE AND WEIGHT CONTROL DEVICE, ATOM! IT WILL BOTH SEND AND RECEIVE THE VARIOUS TYPES OF SIGNALS WE HAVE!
WONDERFUL!

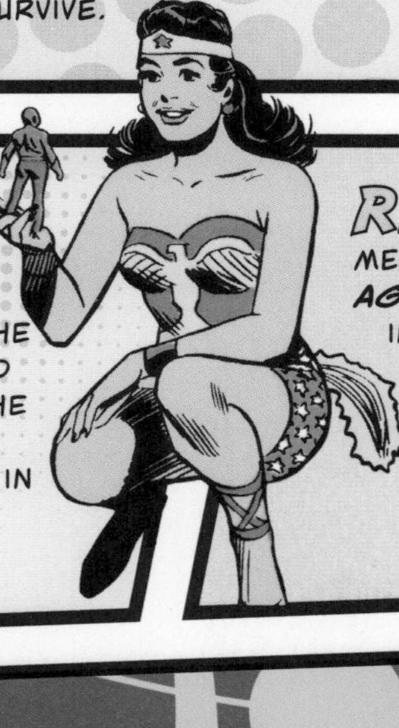

THE ***NEW ATOM*** FIRST APPEARED IN ***SHOWCASE #34*** (OCTOBER 1961). THE CHARACTER PROVED SO POPULAR THAT HE RECEIVED HIS OWN SELF-TITLED BOOK IN JULY 1962.

RAY PALMER WOULD MEET HIS ***GOLDEN-AGE COUNTERPART*** IN THE STORY "***CRISIS ON EARTH-ONE!***" FROM ***JUSTICE LEAGUE OF AMERICA #21*** (AUGUST 1963).

THE ATOM HAD AN ***ECLECTIC GROUP OF FOES***, INCLUDING THE TIME THIEF KNOWN AS ***CHRONOS*** AND ***JASON WOODRUE***, WHO WOULD ONE DAY BECOME THE DEADLY ***FLORONIC MAN***.

SHOWCASE #34
OCTOBER 1961
ART BY GIL KANE, MURPHY ANDERSON

AQUAMAN™

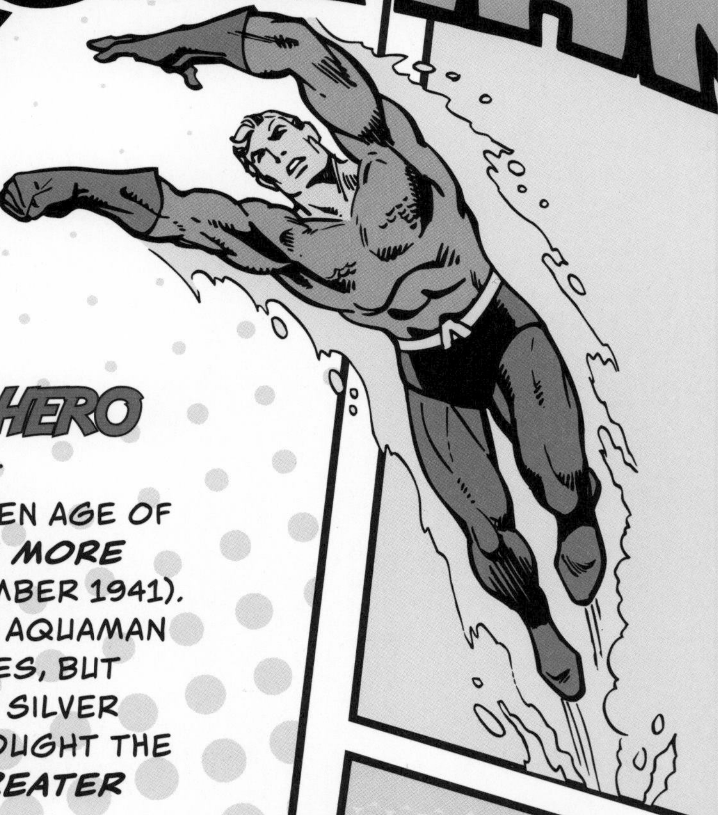

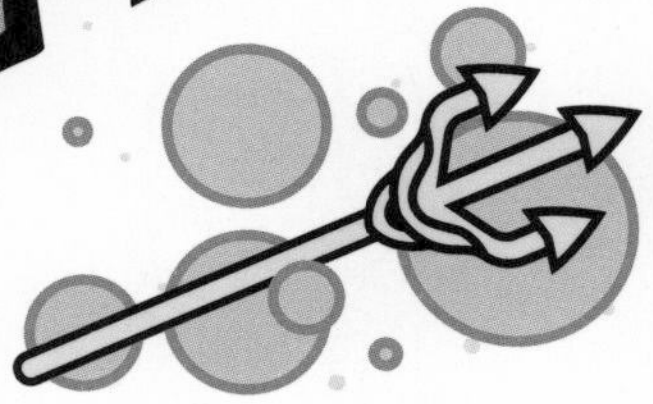

THE UNDERSEA HERO

AQUAMAN MADE HIS FIRST APPEARANCE IN THE GOLDEN AGE OF COMICS, IN THE PAGES OF ***MORE FUN COMICS #73*** (NOVEMBER 1941). THROUGHOUT THE 1940S, AQUAMAN APPEARED IN MANY STORIES, BUT IT WAS HIS REVIVAL IN THE SILVER AGE OF COMICS THAT BROUGHT THE SUPER HERO TO ***EVEN GREATER RECOGNITION.***

ADVENTURE COMICS #260 (MAY 1959) WOULD REVEAL THAT AQUAMAN'S ***TRUE NAME*** WAS ARTHUR CURRY. HE WAS THE SON OF A LIGHTHOUSE KEEPER NAMED THOMAS CURRY, WHO WAS A HUMAN, AND AN OUTCAST FROM THE ***UNDERWATER CITY OF ATLANTIS*** NAMED ATLANNA. YOUNG ARTHUR LEARNED THAT HE COULD ***SURVIVE UNDERWATER*** AND COMMUNICATE WITH SEA CREATURES. HE WOULD GO ON TO ASSUME THE IDENTITY OF ***AQUAMAN.***

AS WITH THE OTHER REVIVALS OF ***GOLDEN AGE DC SUPER HEROES,*** AQUAMAN WOULD PROVE POPULAR WITH READERS, AND SOON HE HAD A TITLE OF HIS OWN. ***AQUAMAN #1*** ARRIVED IN FEBRUARY 1962, AS CURRY AND HIS YOUNG PROTÉGÉ, AQUALAD, TEAM UP WITH A WATER SPRITE NAMED QUISP TO TACKLE THE FIRE-TROLLS SEEKING TO ***ATTACK THE SURFACE WORLD.***

WITH THE HELP OF TOPO THE OCTOPUS, AQUAMAN AND HIS FRIENDS MANAGE TO THWART THE FIRE-TROLLS, SAVE THE SURFACE WORLD, AND USHER IN A NEW ERA OF ***UNDERSEA ADVENTURE.***

AQUAMAN

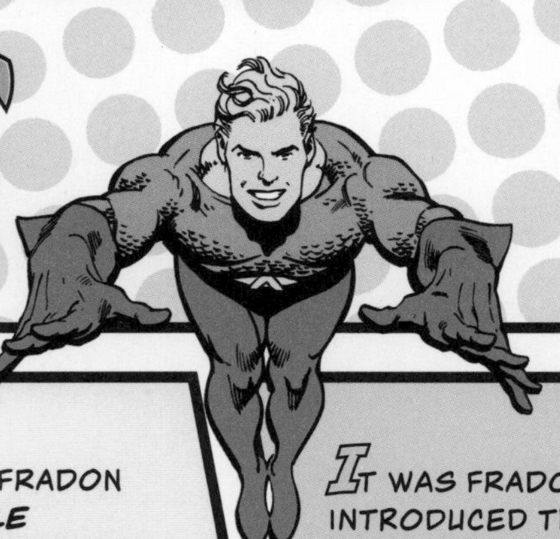

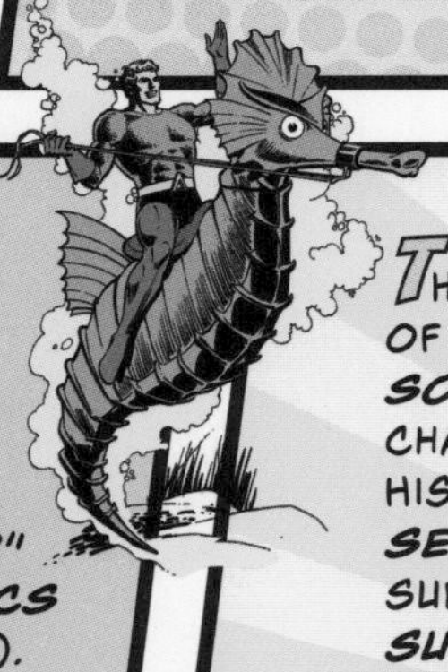

ARTIST RAMONA FRADON LEFT AN ***INDELIBLE STAMP*** ON AQUAMAN WITH AN AMAZING RUN ON THE CHARACTER FROM 1951 THROUGH 1961 IN THE PAGES OF ***ADVENTURE COMICS.***

IT WAS FRADON WHO INTRODUCED THE CHARACTER OF TOPO THE OCTOPUS IN THE STORY "***AQUAMAN'S UNDERSEA PARTNER***" IN ***ADVENTURE COMICS #229*** (OCTOBER 1956).

THE 1960S REVIVAL OF AQUAMAN PROVED ***SO POPULAR*** THAT THE CHARACTER RECEIVED HIS VERY OWN ***ANIMATED SERIES*** IN 1967, ALONGSIDE SUPERMAN IN THE ***SUPERMAN/AQUAMAN HOUR OF ADVENTURE.***

AQUAMAN / STICKERS ON PAGE 77. SOLUTION ON PAGE 49.

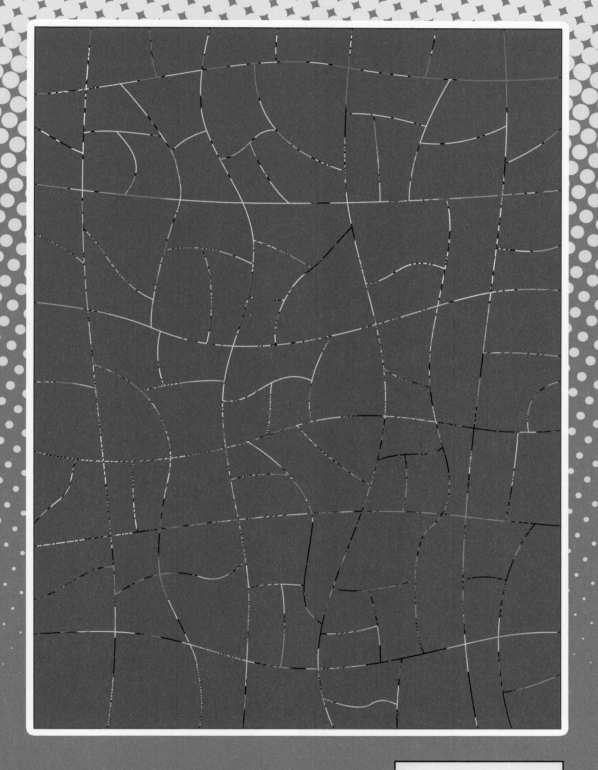

AQUAMAN #1
FEBRUARY 1962
ART BY NICK CARDY

HAWKMAN™

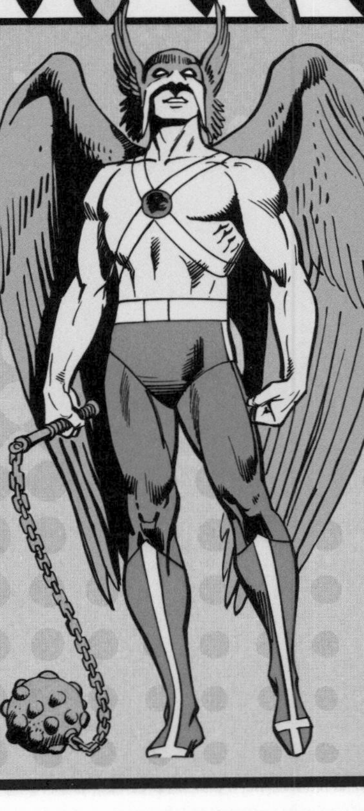

LIKE GREEN LANTERN,

THE FLASH, AND THE ATOM, HAWKMAN ALSO HAD HIS ROOTS IN THE ***GOLDEN AGE OF COMICS***. MAKING HIS FIRST APPEARANCE IN ***FLASH COMICS #1*** (JANUARY 1940), THE FIRST INCARNATION OF HAWKMAN WAS ARCHAEOLOGIST CARTER HALL, WHO DISCOVERED THAT HE WAS THE REINCARNATION OF THE ***EGYPTIAN PRINCE KHUFU***. USING THE RARE "NINTH METAL" (LATER CALLED NTH METAL) WITH ***ANTI-GRAVITATIONAL*** PROPERTIES, HALL CREATED A PAIR OF WINGS. WEARING A MASK OF THE EGYPTIAN HAWK GOD, HALL BECAME ***HAWKMAN***.

WHEN IT CAME TIME TO REVIVE THE CHARACTER IN THE ***SILVER AGE***, WRITER GARDNER FOX AND ARTIST JOE KUBERT REIMAGINED HAWKMAN AS AN ***ALIEN POLICE OFFICER*** FROM THE PLANET THANAGAR NAMED KATAR HOL. HOL AND HIS WIFE SHAYERA HAD COME TO EARTH IN PURSUIT OF A ***THANAGARIAN CRIMINAL*** AND DECIDED TO STAY AND STUDY THE METHODS OF EARTH'S POLICE OFFICERS.

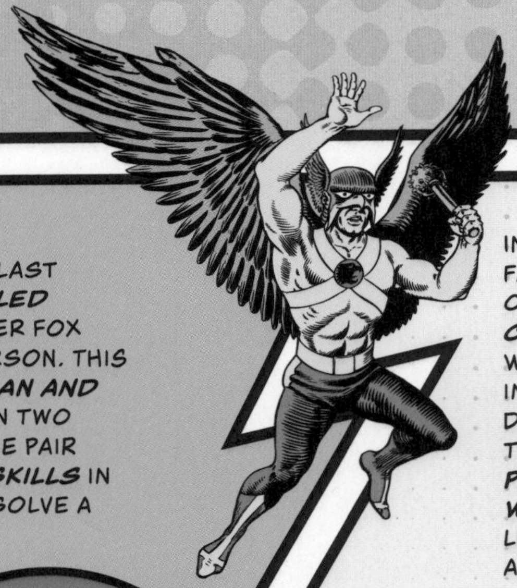

IN MAY OF 1964, HAWKMAN AT LAST RECEIVED HIS OWN ***SELF-TITLED SERIES***, WRITTEN BY GARDNER FOX AND DRAWN BY MURPHY ANDERSON. THIS NEW INCARNATION OF ***HAWKMAN AND HAWKGIRL*** WERE FEATURED IN TWO ADVENTURES. IN THE FIRST, THE PAIR CHALLENGED THEIR ***POLICE SKILLS*** IN A FRIENDLY COMPETITION TO SOLVE A MUSEUM ROBBERY.

IN THE SECOND, THE DUO FACED CHAC, THE LEADER OF AN ***ANCIENT AZTEC CIVILIZATION*** WHO REVIVED IN PRESENT DAY, TRYING TO UNCOVER ***POWERFUL WEAPONS*** LEFT BEHIND BY ALIENS.

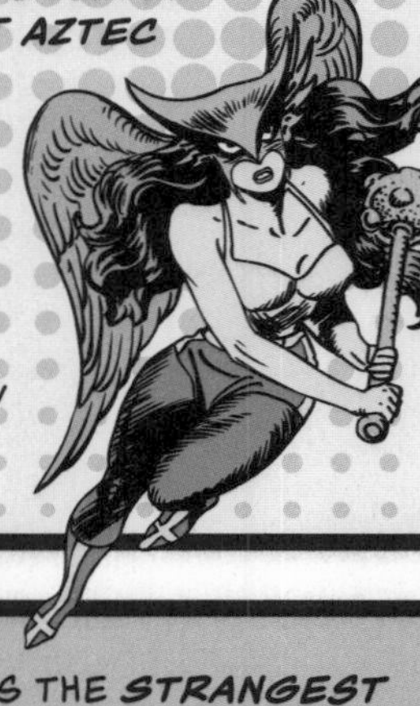

THE NAME "***KATAR HOL***" WAS INTENDED AS AN HOMAGE TO THE GOLDEN AGE HAWKMAN'S ***SECRET IDENTITY***, "CARTER HALL."

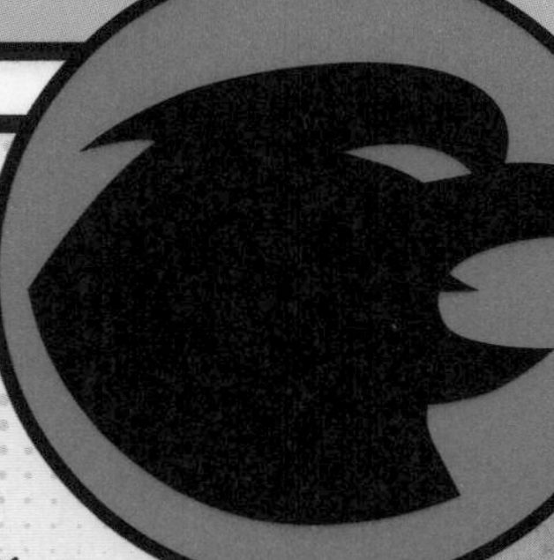

THE ***SILVER AGE HAWKMAN*** WOULD BECOME A MEMBER OF THE ***JUSTICE LEAGUE*** WITH ISSUE #31 OF ***JUSTICE LEAGUE OF AMERICA*** (NOVEMBER 1964).

PERHAPS THE ***STRANGEST FOE*** FACED BY HAWKMAN AND HAWKGIRL CAME IN THE FORM OF CARL SANDS, ***THE SHADOW THIEF***. THANKS TO AN ALIEN DEVICE CALLED THE ***DIMENSIONMETER***, SANDS WAS ABLE TO TRANSFORM HIMSELF INTO A ***LIVING SHADOW***.

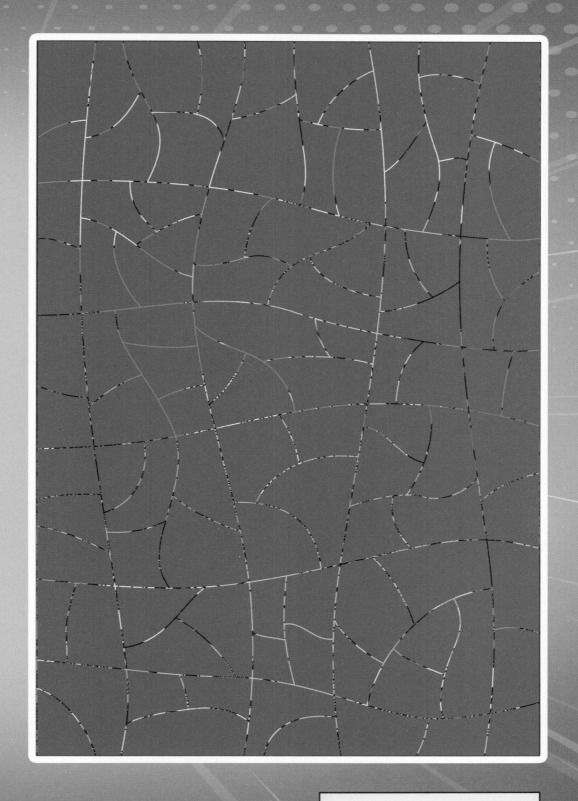

HAWKMAN #1
MAY 1964
ART BY MURPHY ANDERSON

JUSTICE LEAGUE AMERICA

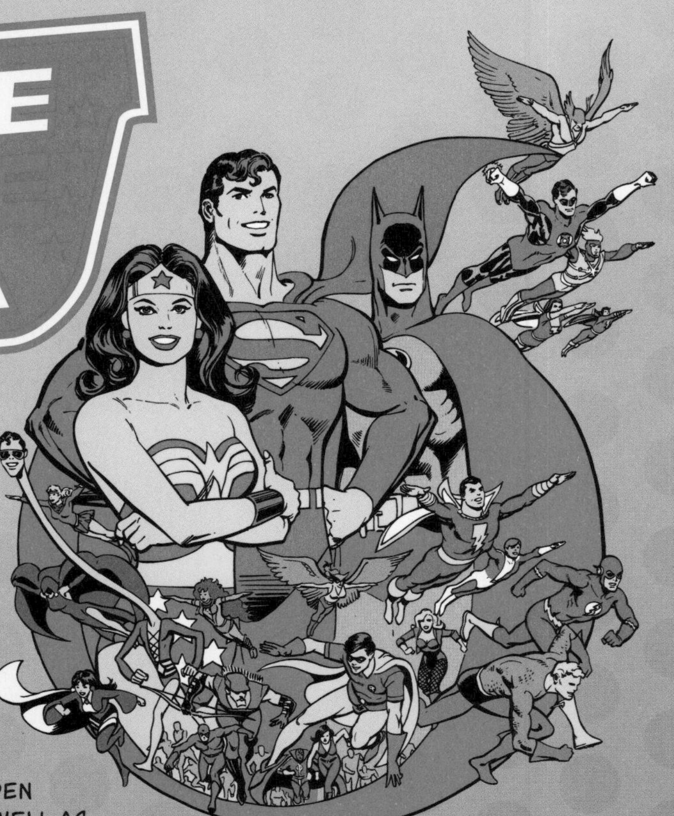

THE CONCEPT WAS BRILLIANT–

TAKE THE BRAND'S ***SUPER HEROES***, PUT THEM ALL ON A ***TEAM***, AND TELL STORIES ABOUT THEIR ***DARING EXPLOITS***. THE APTLY NAMED ***JUSTICE SOCIETY*** MADE ITS FIRST APPEARANCE IN THE PAGES OF ***ALL-STAR COMICS #3*** (DECEMBER 1940). IT FEATURED THE EXPLOITS OF AN A-LIST TEAM THAT INCLUDED THE GOLDEN AGE FLASH, HAWKMAN, GREEN LANTERN, AND ATOM, AS WELL AS THE SPECTRE, HOURMAN, THE SANDMAN, DOCTOR FATE, AND JOHNNY THUNDER AND THUNDERBOLT.

NOTABLY ABSENT FROM THE PROCEEDINGS WERE SUPERMAN, BATMAN, AND WONDER WOMAN. BOTH SUPERMAN AND BATMAN WERE CONSIDERED ***FOUNDING MEMBERS OF THE JUSTICE SOCIETY***, BUT THEY RARELY MADE APPEARANCES. THIS WAS PARTLY DUE TO THE FACT THAT EACH HERO HAD TWO COMIC BOOKS DEDICATED TO THEIR OWN ADVENTURES: ***ACTION COMICS*** AND ***SUPERMAN***, AND ***DETECTIVE COMICS*** AND ***BATMAN***.

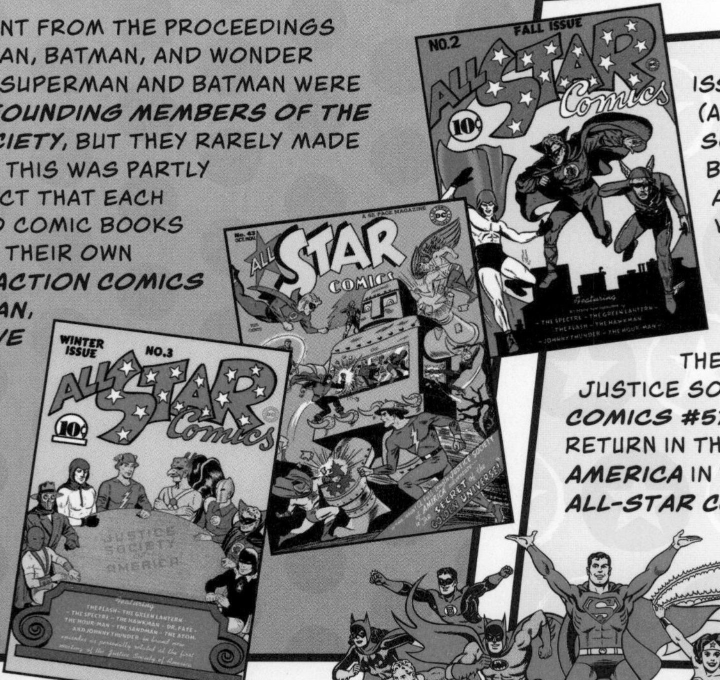
NO.2
FALL ISSUE
ALL STAR Comics
10¢
STAR
WINTER ISSUE
NO.3
ALL STAR Comics
10¢
JUSTICE SOCIETY OF AMERICA

ISSUE #36 OF ***ALL-STAR COMICS*** (AUGUST 1947) PROVED TO BE SOMETHING SPECIAL. SUPERMAN, BATMAN, AND WONDER WOMAN WERE ALL INVOLVED IN THE ADVENTURE WITH THE JUSTICE SOCIETY. BUT IT ALSO MARKED THE ***FIRST TIME*** WONDER WOMAN AND SUPERMAN EVER MET!

THE GOLDEN AGE ADVENTURES OF THE JUSTICE SOCIETY WOULD END WITH ***ALL-STAR COMICS #57*** (MARCH 1951). THE TEAM WOULD RETURN IN THE PAGES OF ***JUSTICE LEAGUE OF AMERICA*** IN THE 1960S AND THEN IN A REVIVED ***ALL-STAR COMICS*** IN THE 1970S.

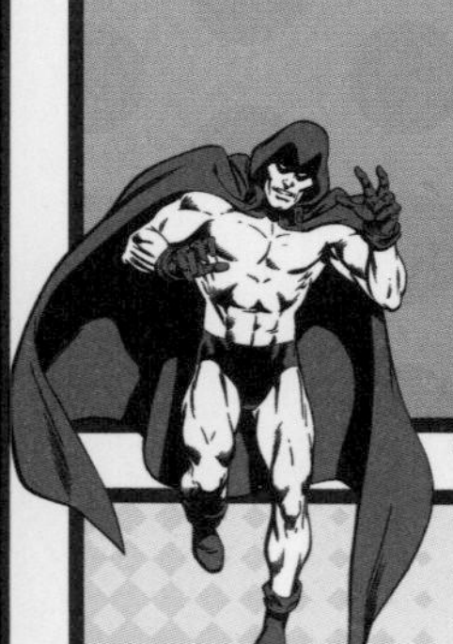

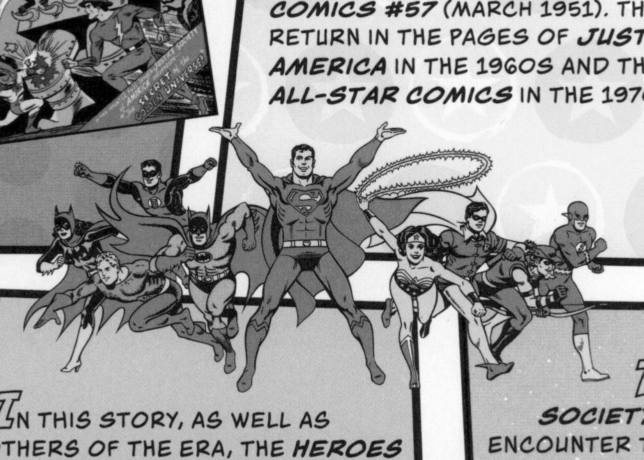

ALL THE STORIES THAT COMPRISED ***ALL-STAR COMICS #36*** WERE WRITTEN BY GARDNER FOX AND ILLUSTRATED BY A WHO'S WHO OF COMIC ARTISTS THAT INCLUDED JOE KUBERT AND IRWIN HASEN.

IN THIS STORY, AS WELL AS OTHERS OF THE ERA, THE ***HEROES OF THE JUSTICE SOCIETY*** HAD NO CLUE THAT BRUCE WAYNE WAS SECRETLY BATMAN--EXCEPT FOR SUPERMAN, THAT IS. BOTH HE AND THE MAN OF STEEL KNEW ONE ANOTHER'S CIVILIAN IDENTITIES.

THE JUSTICE SOCIETY WOULD ENCOUNTER THEIR SILVER AGE DESCENDANTS IN THE STORY ***"CRISIS ON EARTH-ONE,"*** FROM ***JUSTICE LEAGUE OF AMERICA #21*** (AUGUST 1963). THIS MARKED THE FIRST RETURN APPEARANCE OF THE JUSTICE SOCIETY SINCE 1951.

STICKERS ON PAGE 81. SOLUTION ON PAGE 51.

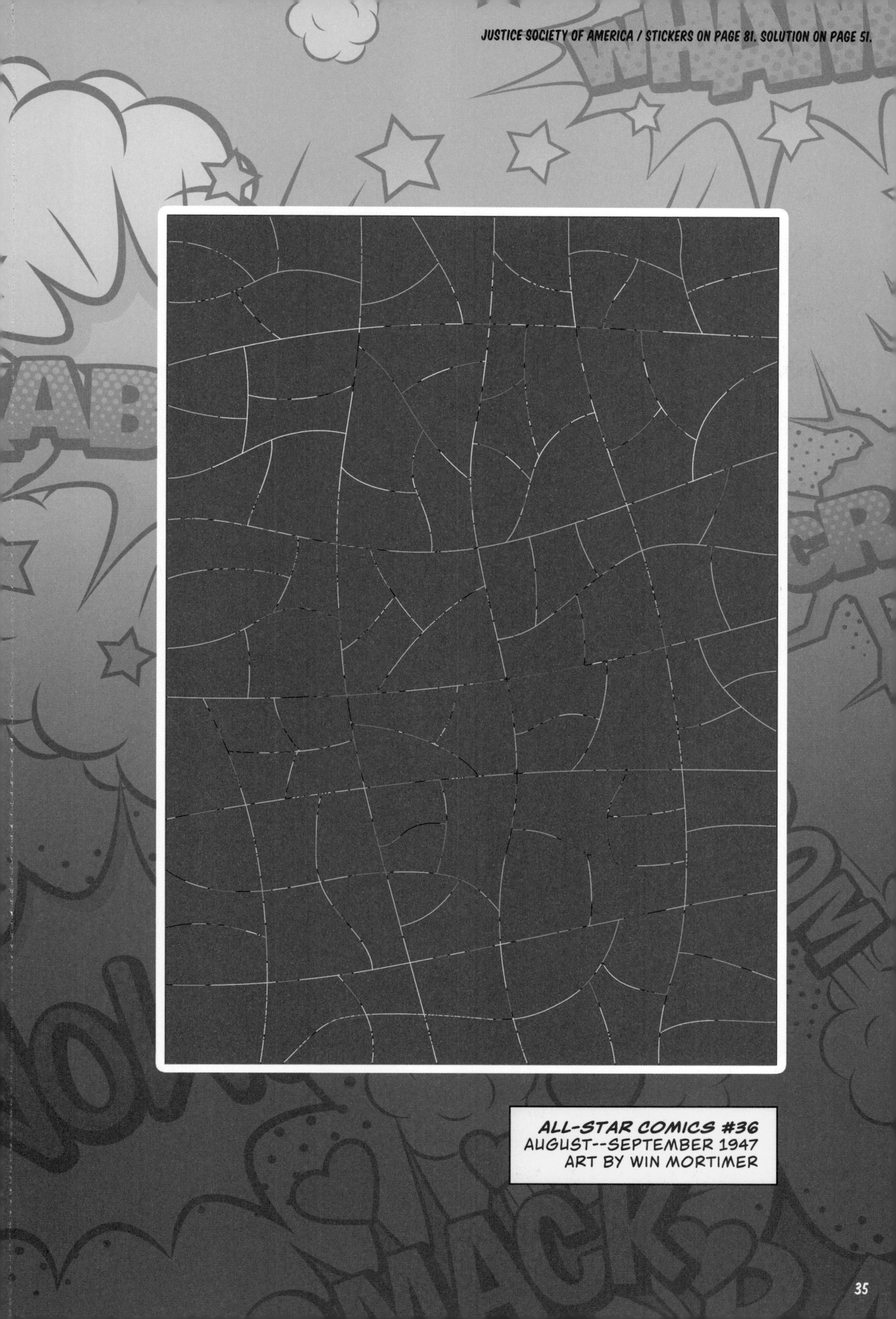

ALL-STAR COMICS #36
AUGUST--SEPTEMBER 1947
ART BY WIN MORTIMER

SOLUTIONS

The newest of the 'DC' magazines
NO.1 JANUARY
SENSATION COMICS
DC COMICS ORIGINALS
10¢
Featuring THE SENSATIONAL NEW ADVENTURE STRIP CHARACTER-
Wonder Woman!

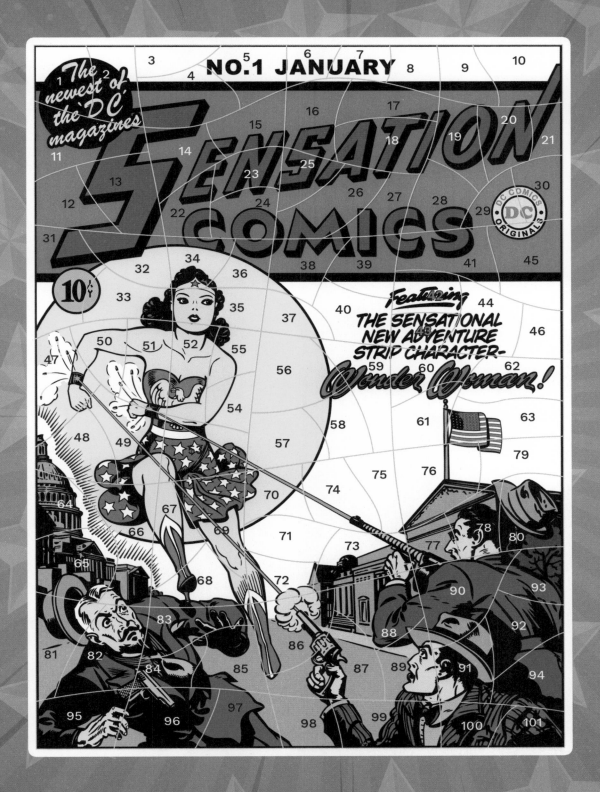

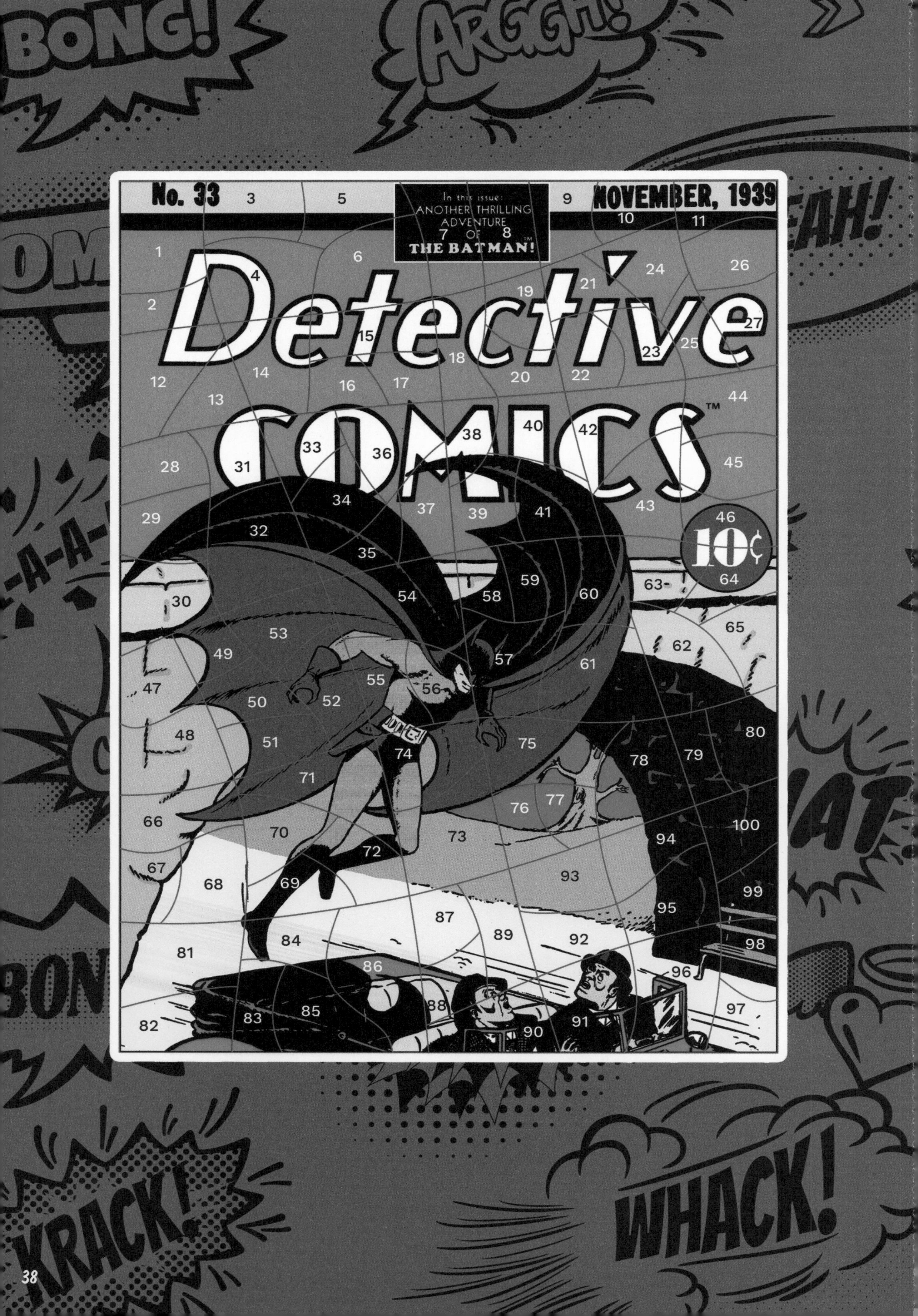
BONG!
ARGGH!
No. 33
In this issue: ANOTHER THRILLING ADVENTURE OF THE BATMAN!
NOVEMBER, 1939
Detective COMICS™
10¢
KRACK!
WHACK!

SUPERMAN
NO.23
ACTION
COMICS
GRAND

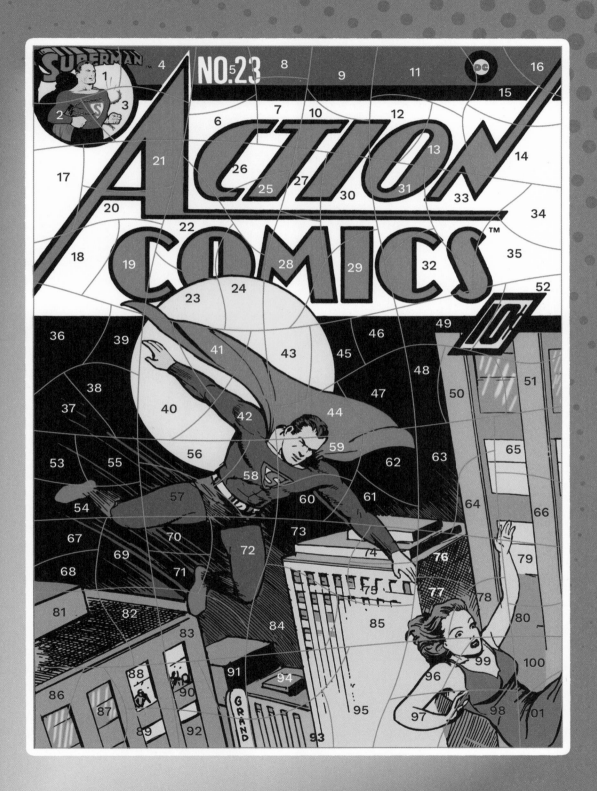

No. 38
The BATMAN
DC PUBLICATION
Detective
COMICS
APRIL
10¢
THE Sensational CHARACTER-
FIND OF 1940....
Robin-
THE BOY WONDER

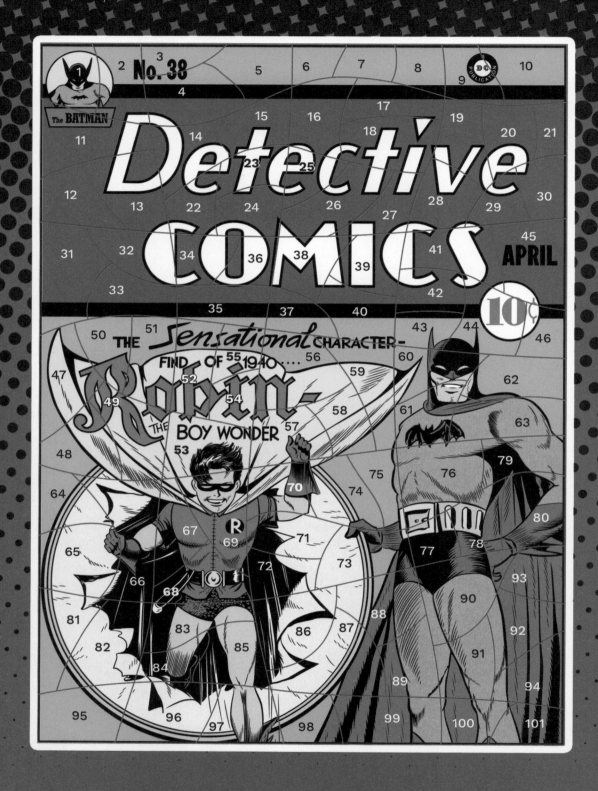

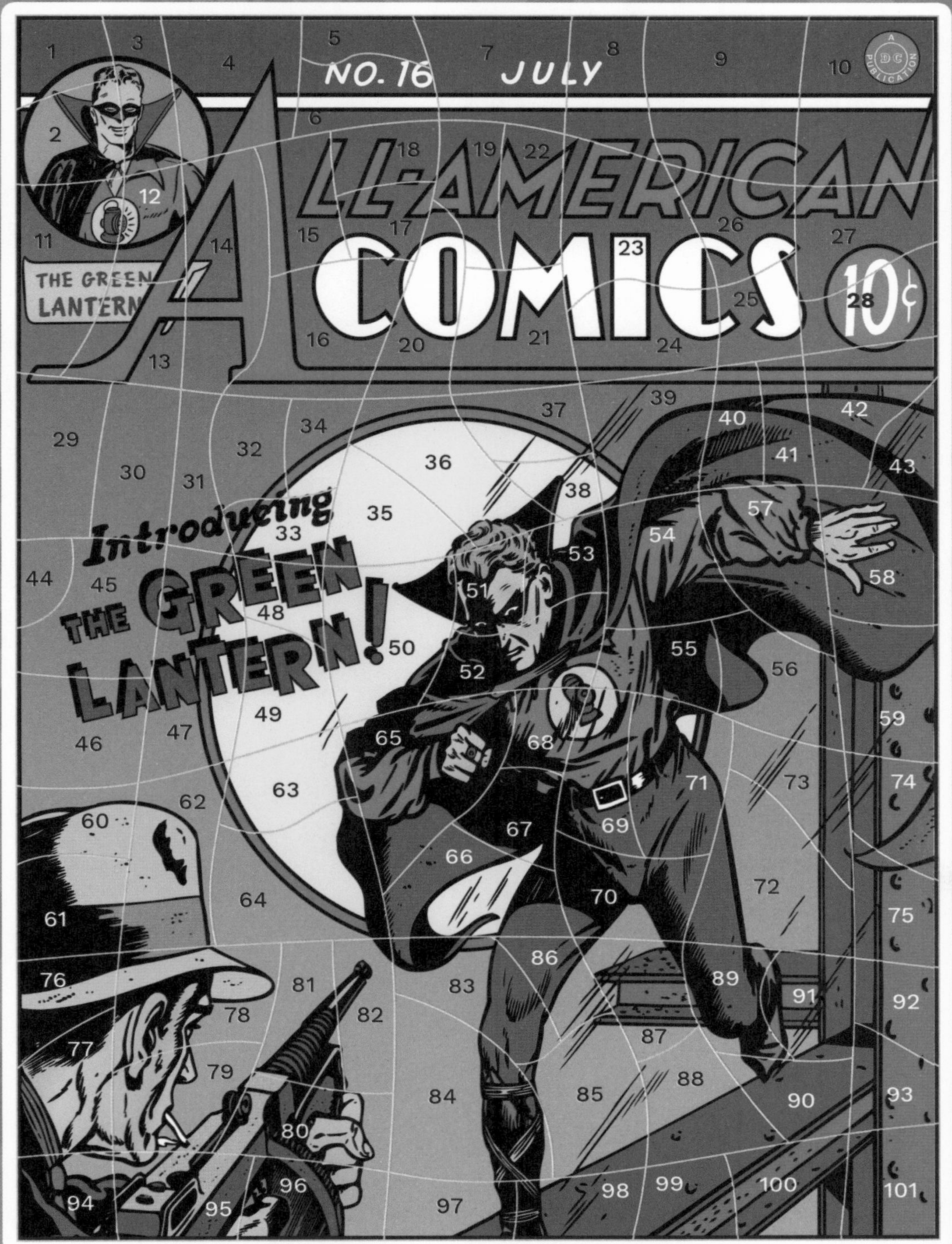
NO. 16
JULY
A DC PUBLICATION
ALL-AMERICAN COMICS
10¢
THE GREEN LANTERN
Introducing THE GREEN LANTERN!

NO. 37
TEN CENTS
BATMAN™
In this issue
THE JOKER™
STEALS THE
BATMAN'S
THUNDER!

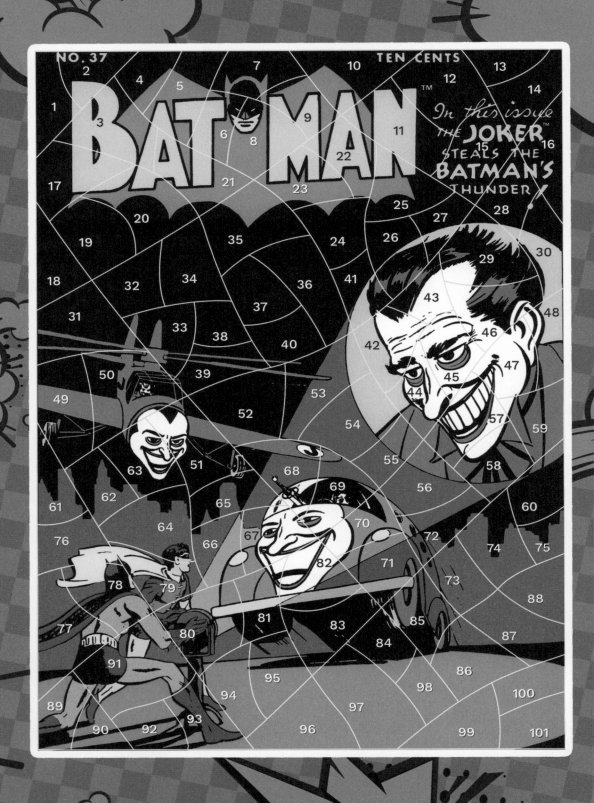

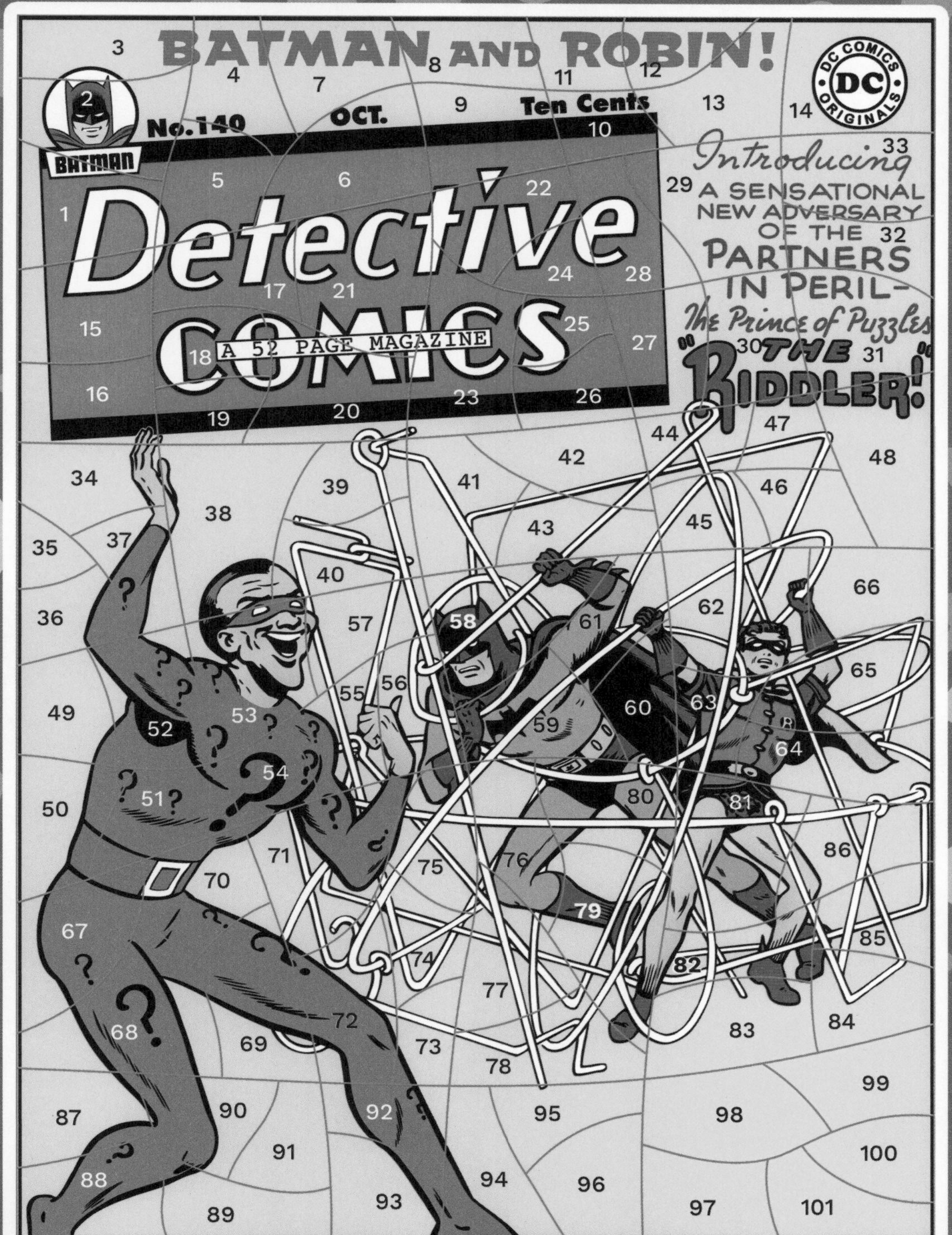
BATMAN AND ROBIN!
No.140
OCT.
Ten Cents
DC COMICS ORIGINALS
BATMAN
Detective COMICS
A 52 PAGE MAGAZINE
Introducing A SENSATIONAL NEW ADVERSARY OF THE PARTNERS IN PERIL-
The Prince of Puzzles
"THE RIDDLER!"

52 BIG PAGES
BATMAN
NO.65
JUNE...JULY
DC COMICS ORIGINALS
DC
10¢
BATMAN
IS THE CATWOMAN AN ALLY OF THE DYNAMIC DUO OR HAS SHE RETURNED TO CRIME? YOU BE THE JURY TO DECIDE, AS GOTHAM CITY BOWS TO...
"THE Empress of the Underworld!"
ROGUES' GALLERY
UNDERCOVER POLICE AGENTS
A-B-C
D-E-F
A-B-C
D-E-F

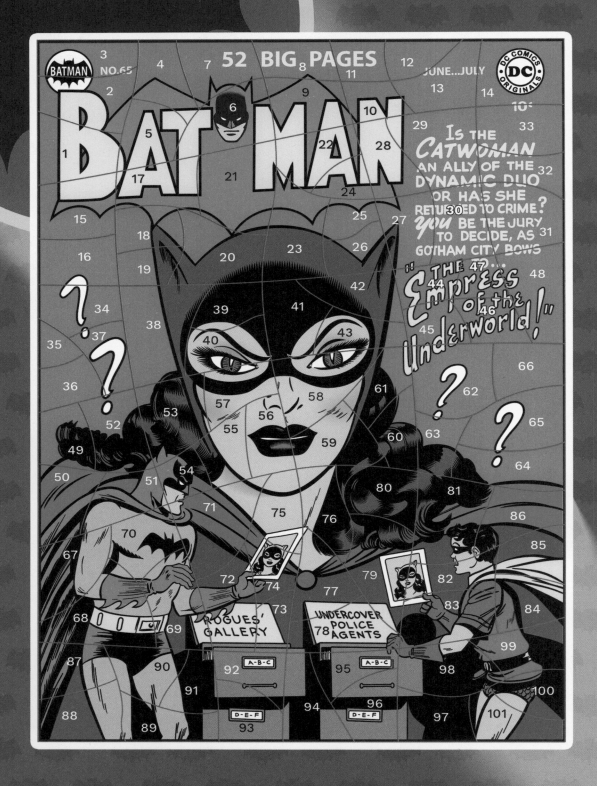

THE FLASH / SOLUTION FOR PAGE 23. STICKERS ON PAGE 69.

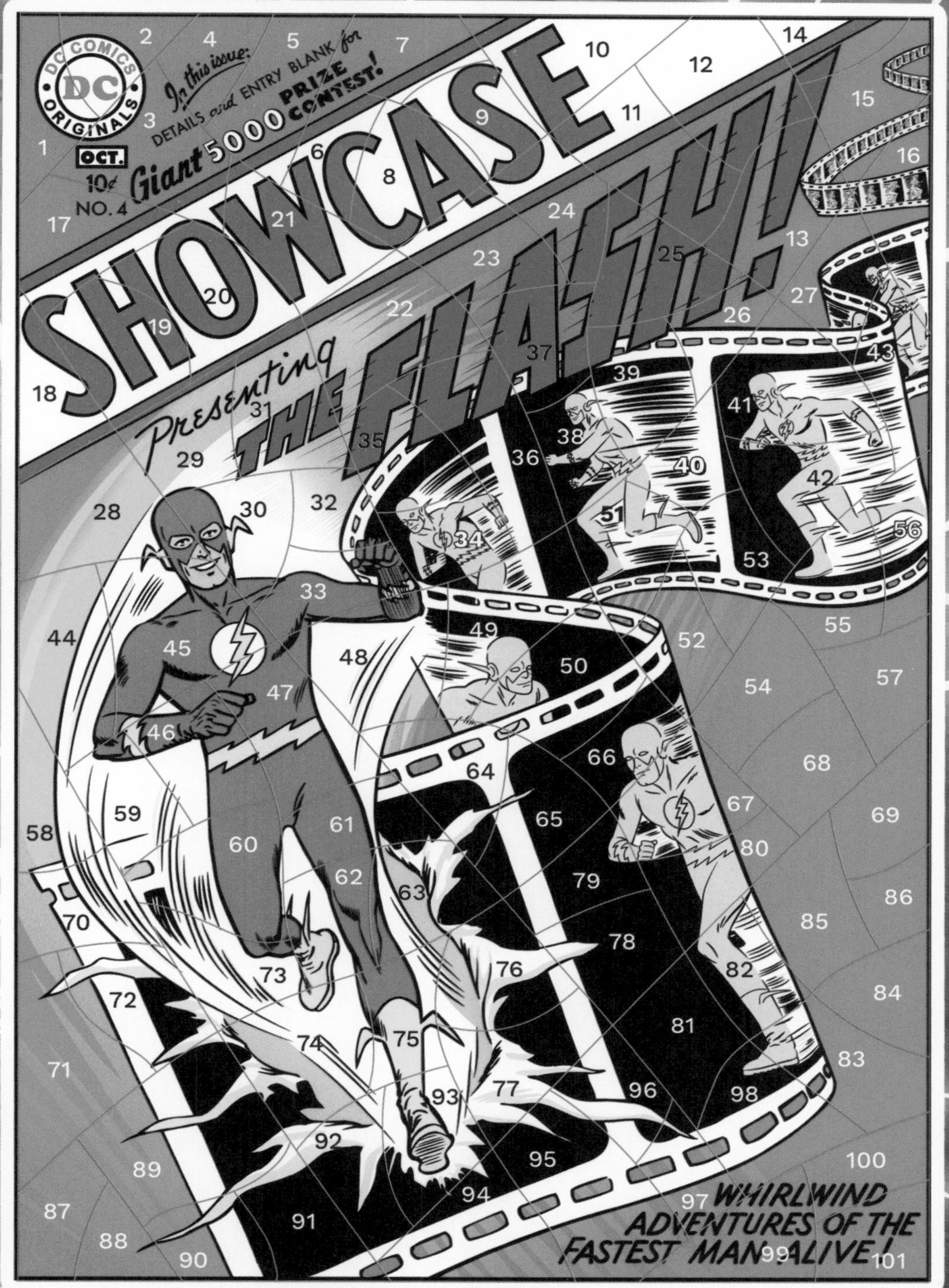
DC COMICS ORIGINALS
DC
OCT.
10¢
NO. 4
In this issue:
DETAILS and ENTRY BLANK for
Giant 5000 PRIZE CONTEST!
SHOWCASE
Presenting
THE FLASH!
WHIRLWIND
ADVENTURES OF THE
FASTEST MAN ALIVE!

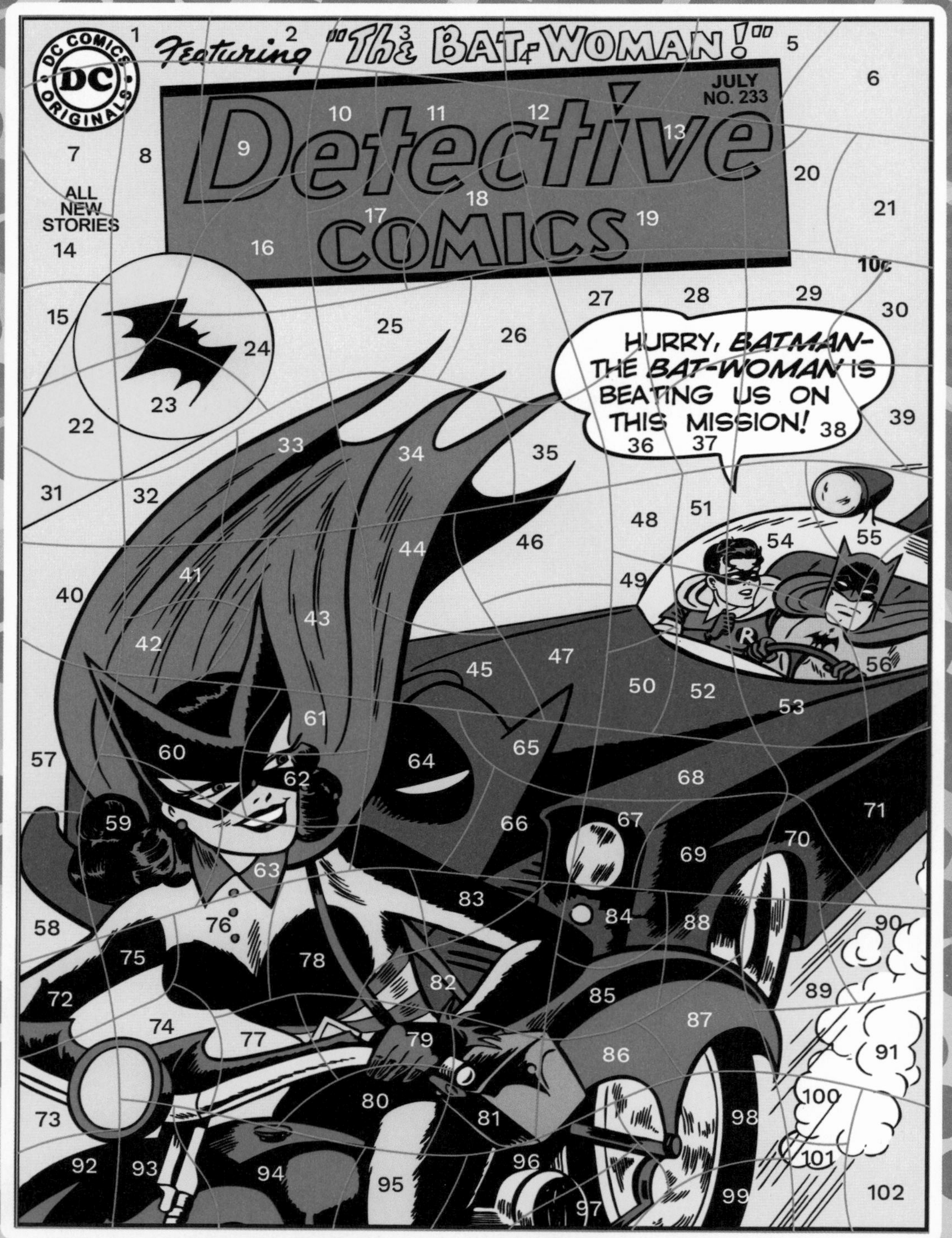
DC COMICS ORIGINALS
DC
Featuring "The BAT-WOMAN!"
JULY NO. 233
Detective COMICS
ALL NEW STORIES
10¢
HURRY, BATMAN- THE BAT-WOMAN IS BEATING US ON THIS MISSION!

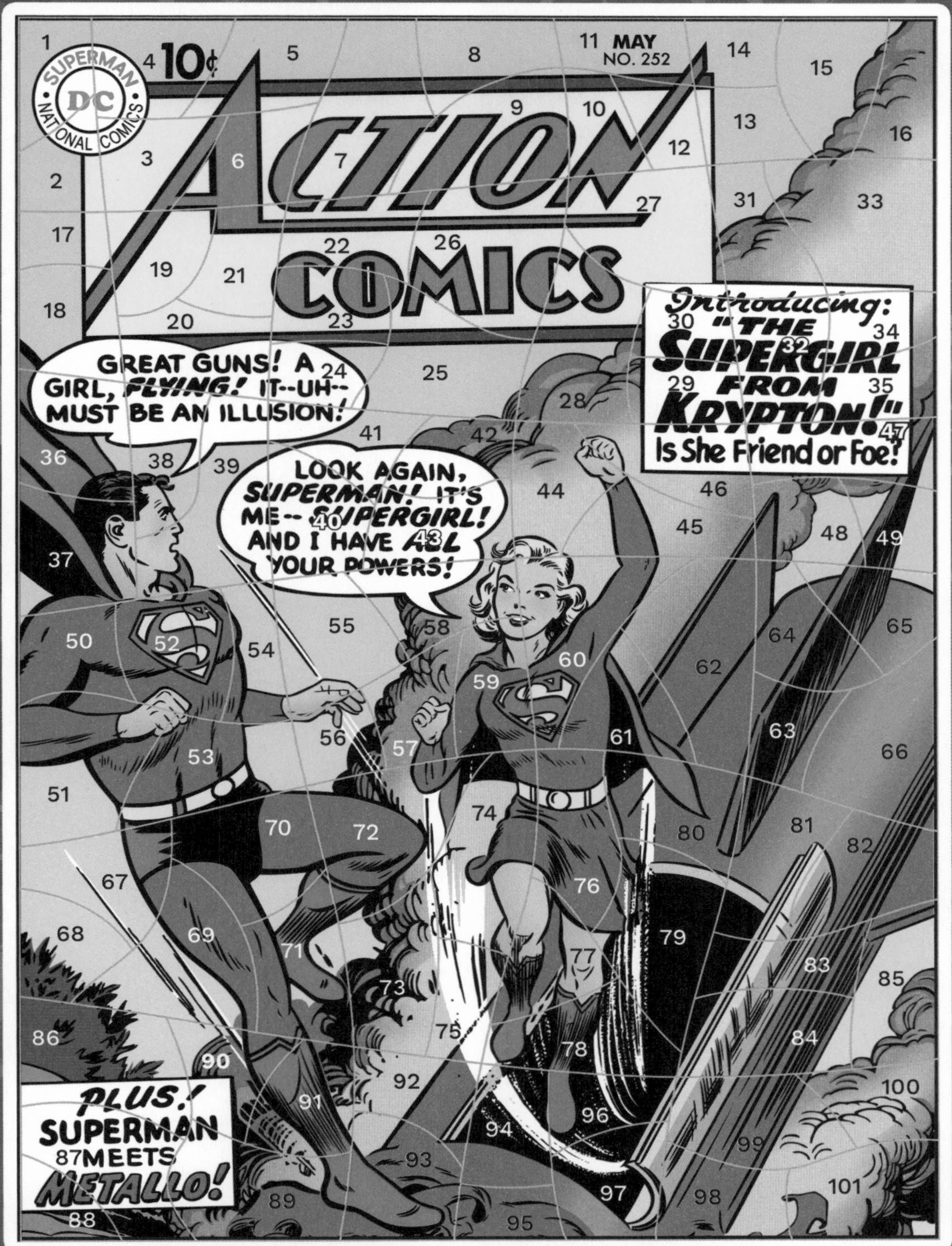
10¢
MAY NO. 252
SUPERMAN DC NATIONAL COMICS
ACTION COMICS
Introducing: "THE SUPERGIRL FROM KRYPTON!" Is She Friend or Foe?
GREAT GUNS! A GIRL, FLYING! IT--UH-- MUST BE AN ILLUSION!
LOOK AGAIN, SUPERMAN! IT'S ME-- SUPERGIRL! AND I HAVE ALL YOUR POWERS!
PLUS! SUPERMAN MEETS METALLO!

DC COMICS ORIGINALS
Introducing THE WORLD'S SMALLEST SUPER-HERO!
SHOWCASE presents
The ATOM
10¢
NO. 34
Featuring "BATTLE of the TINY TITANS!"

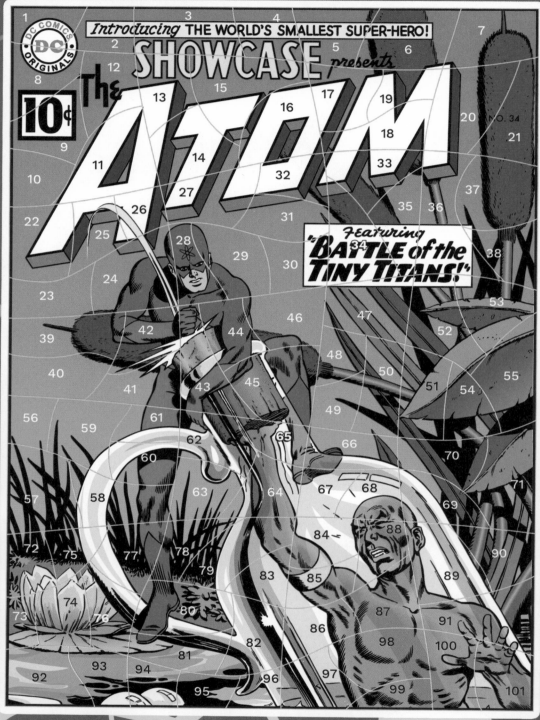

NOW IN A MAGAZINE OF HIS OWN!
DC COMICS ORIGINALS
12¢
FEB.
AQUAMAN
FEATURING THE KING OF THE SEVEN SEAS AND HIS YOUNG ALLY, AQUALAD!
A THRILLING 3-PART NOVEL...
"The INVASION of the FIRE-TROLLS!"
KEEP DODGING, AQUALAD! THOSE FIRE-TROLLS ARE TRYING TO GIVE US AN UNDERWATER HOT-FOOT!

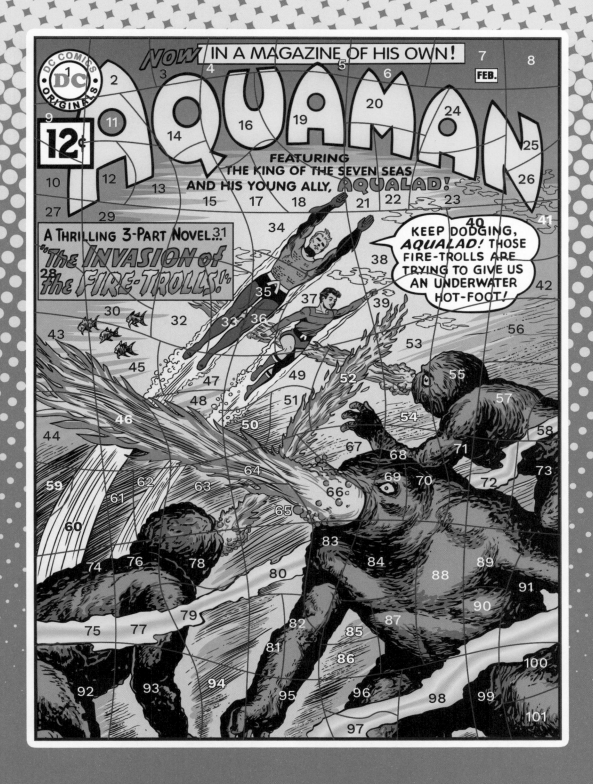

DC COMICS ORIGINALS
DC
12¢
NOW... IN HIS OWN MAGAZINE...
MAY
HAWKMAN
Featuring "MASTER of the SKY-WEAPONS!"

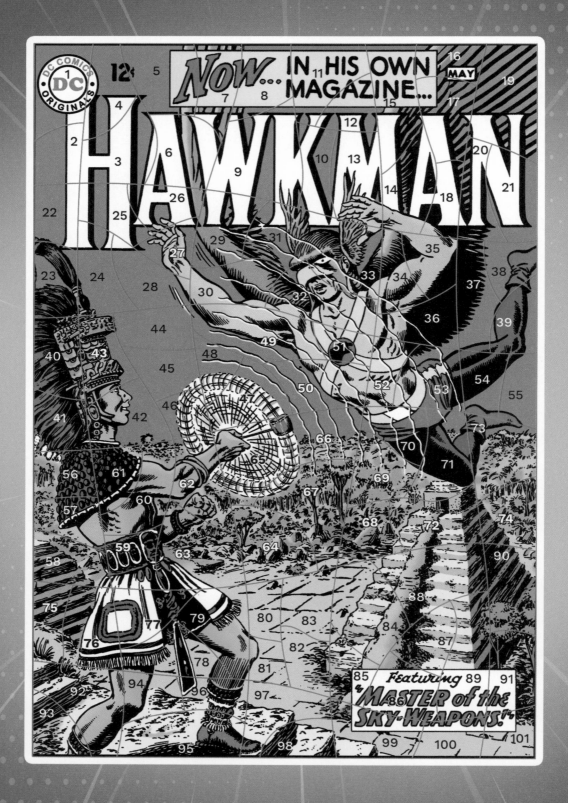

In this issue–SUPERMAN and BATMAN–guest stars!
A SUPERMAN DC PUBLICATION
No.36
AUG.–SEPT.
A 52 PAGE MAGAZINE
TEN CENTS
ALL STAR Comics
JUSTICE SOCIETY OF AMERICA
Another FULL-LENGTH ADVENTURE of the JUSTICE SOCIETY of AMERICA
featuring: THE FLASH, GREEN LANTERN, HAWKMAN, DR. MID-NITE & WONDER WOMAN.
SUPERMAN AND BATMAN GUEST STARS!

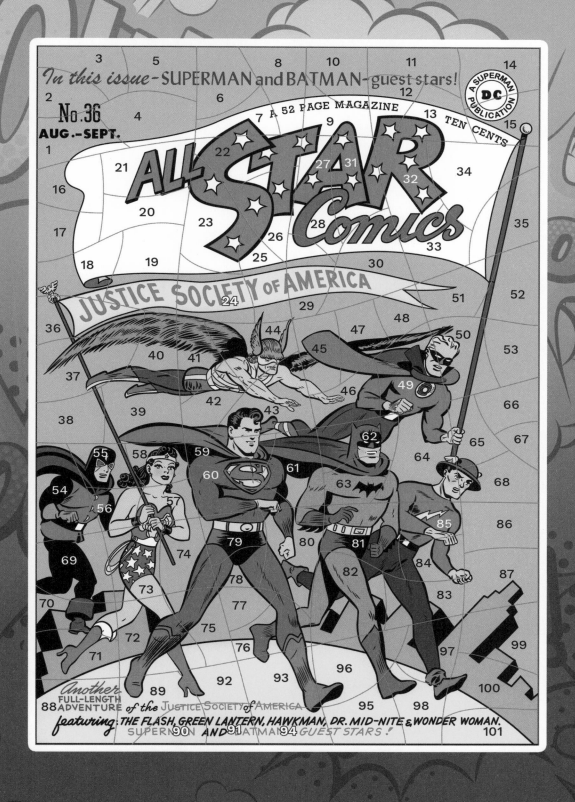

STICKERS

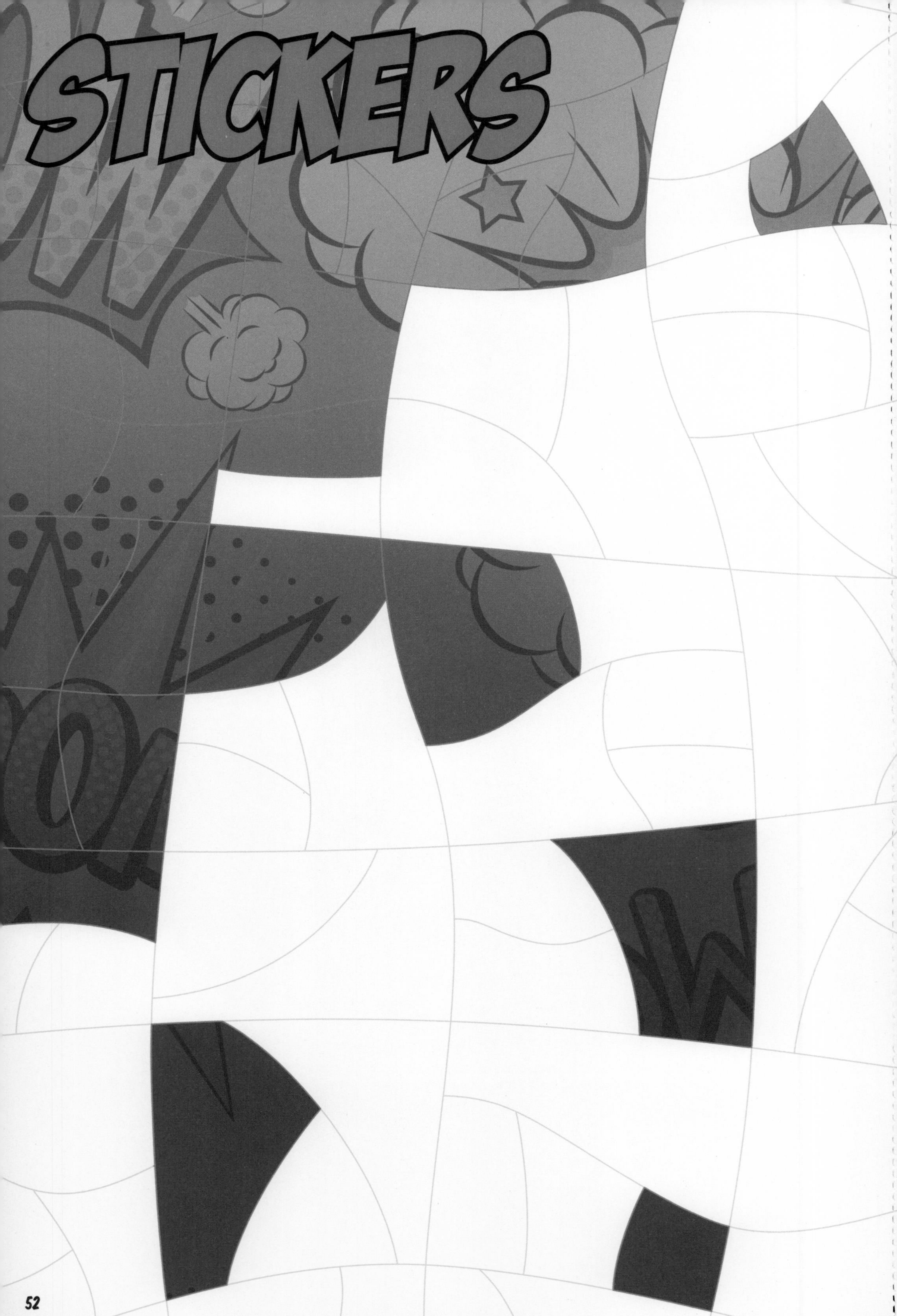

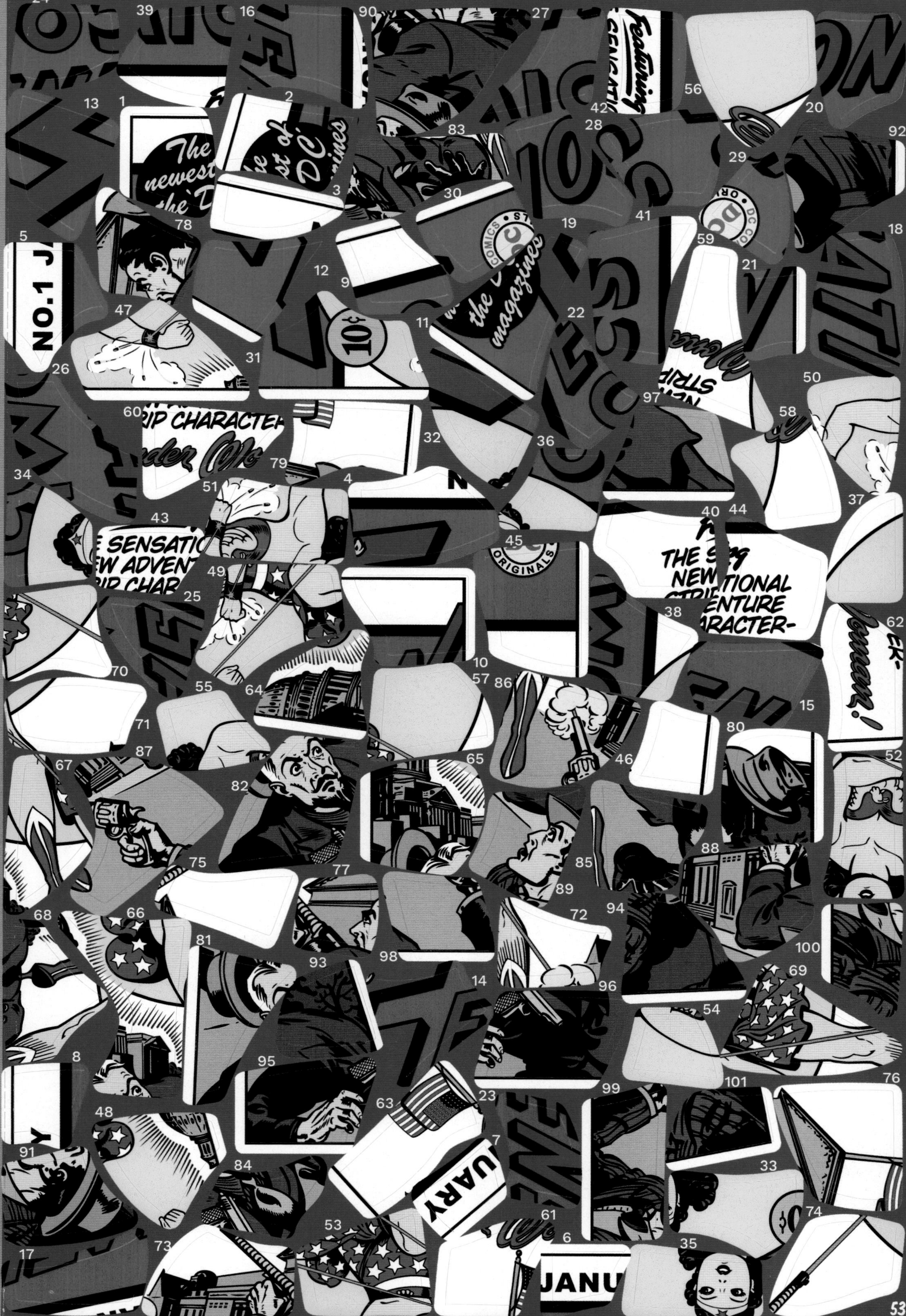
The newest the D
NO.1 JA
RIP CHARACTER
E SENSATIO
W ADVENT
IP CHAR
THE S
NEW TIONAL
ENTURE
ARACTER-
UARY
JANU

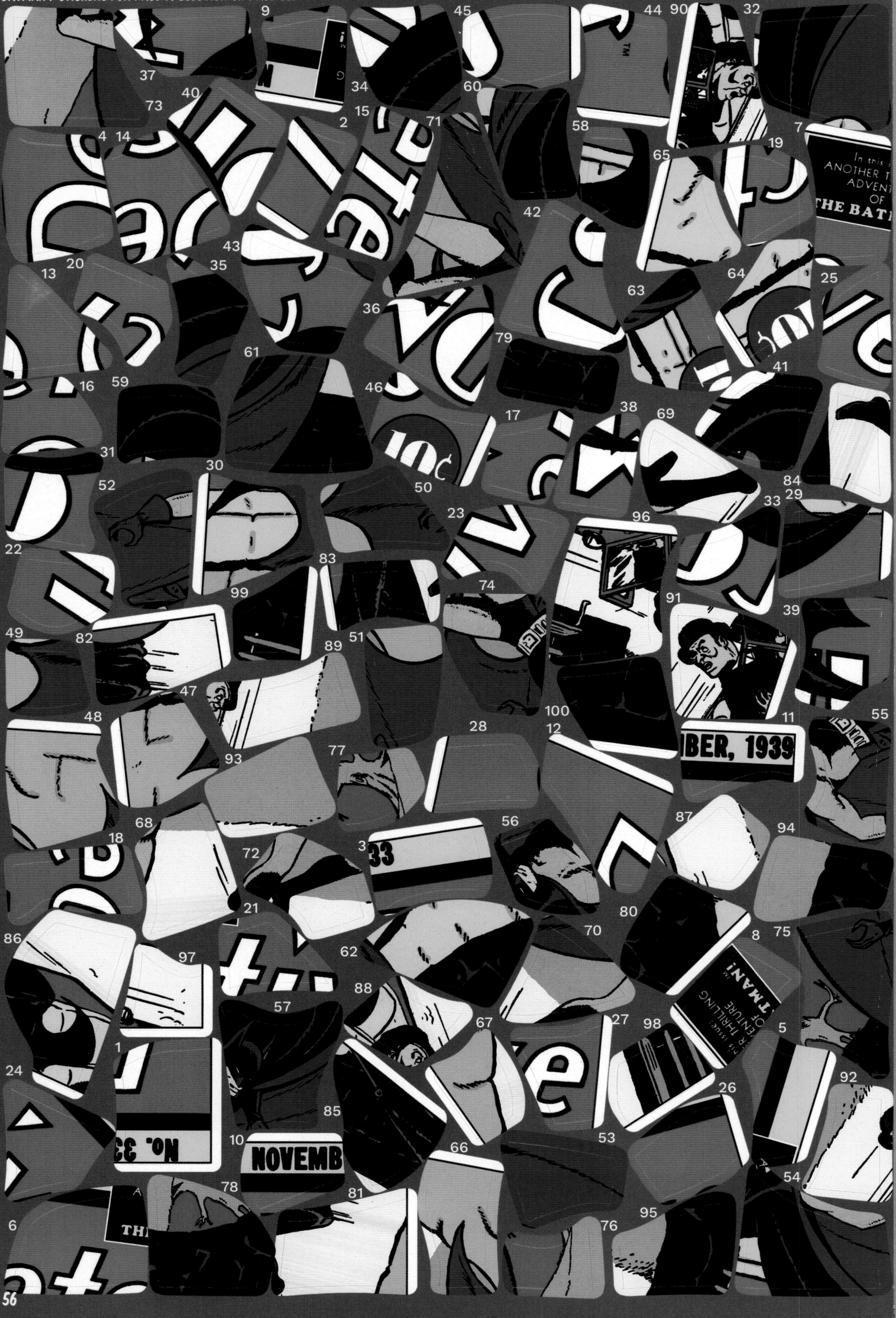
In this
ANOTHER T
ADVENT
OF
THE BAT
BER, 1939
No. 33
NOVEMB

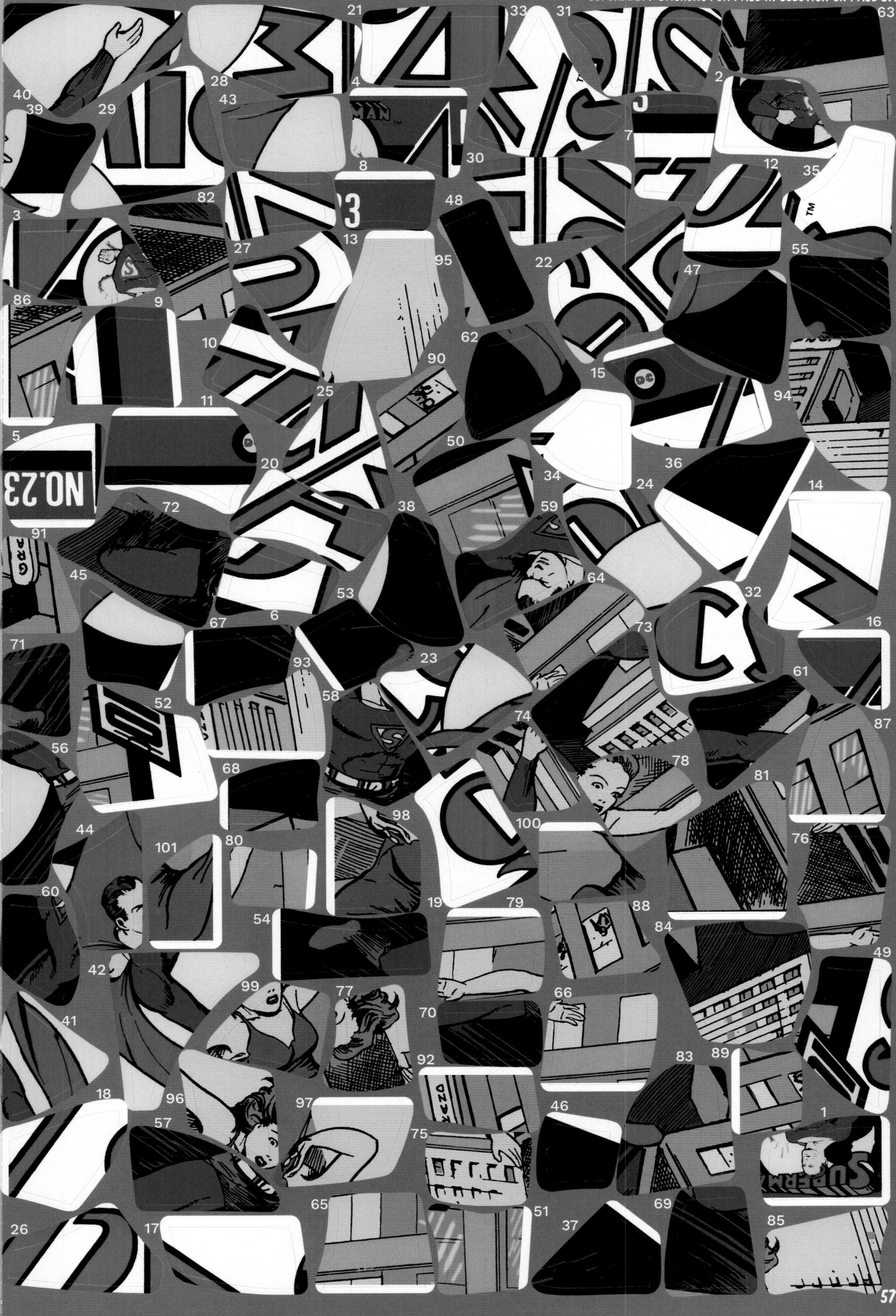
NO.23

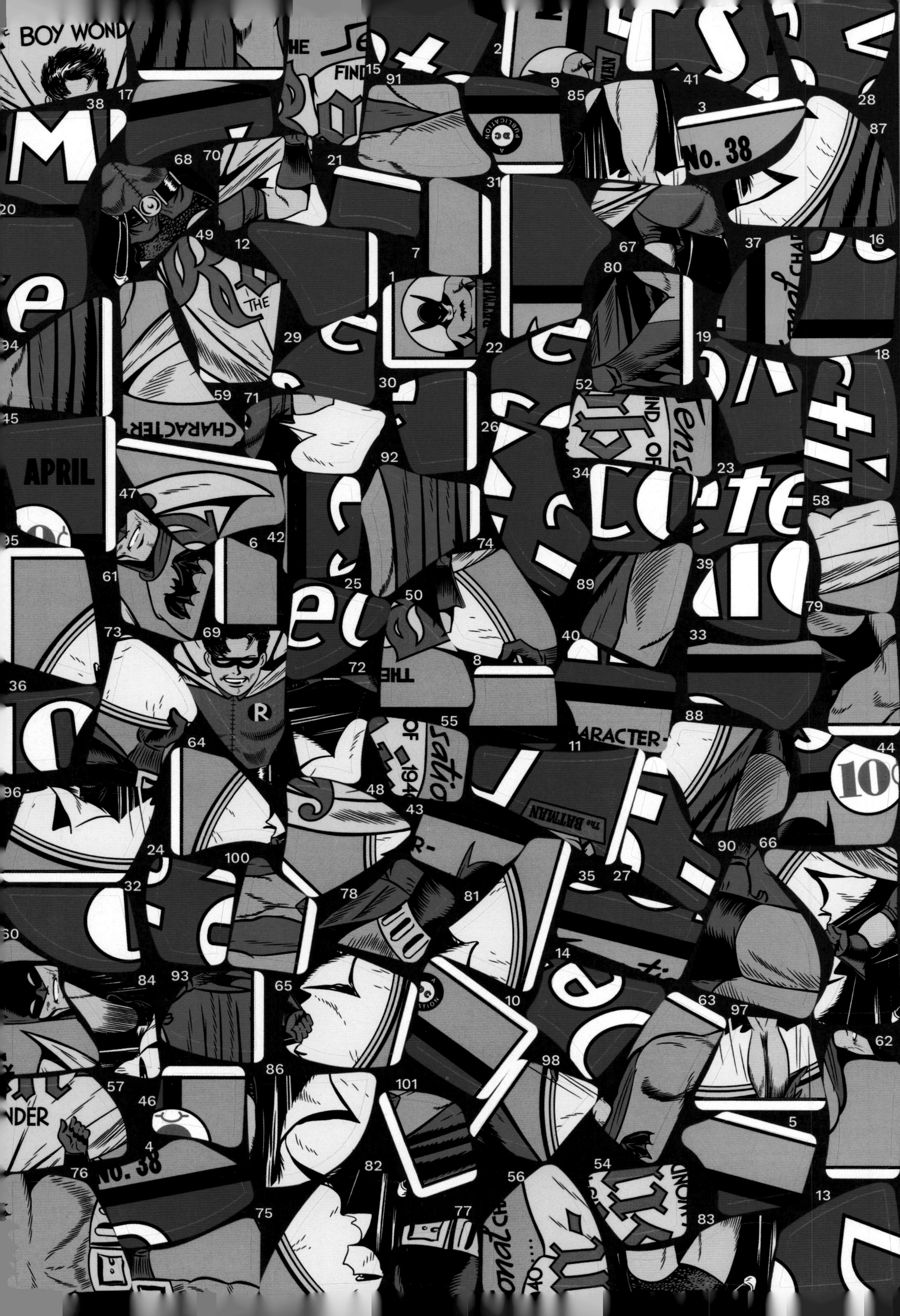
BOY WOND
No. 38
CHARACTER-
APRIL
ARACTER-
The BATMAN
NO. 38
NDER

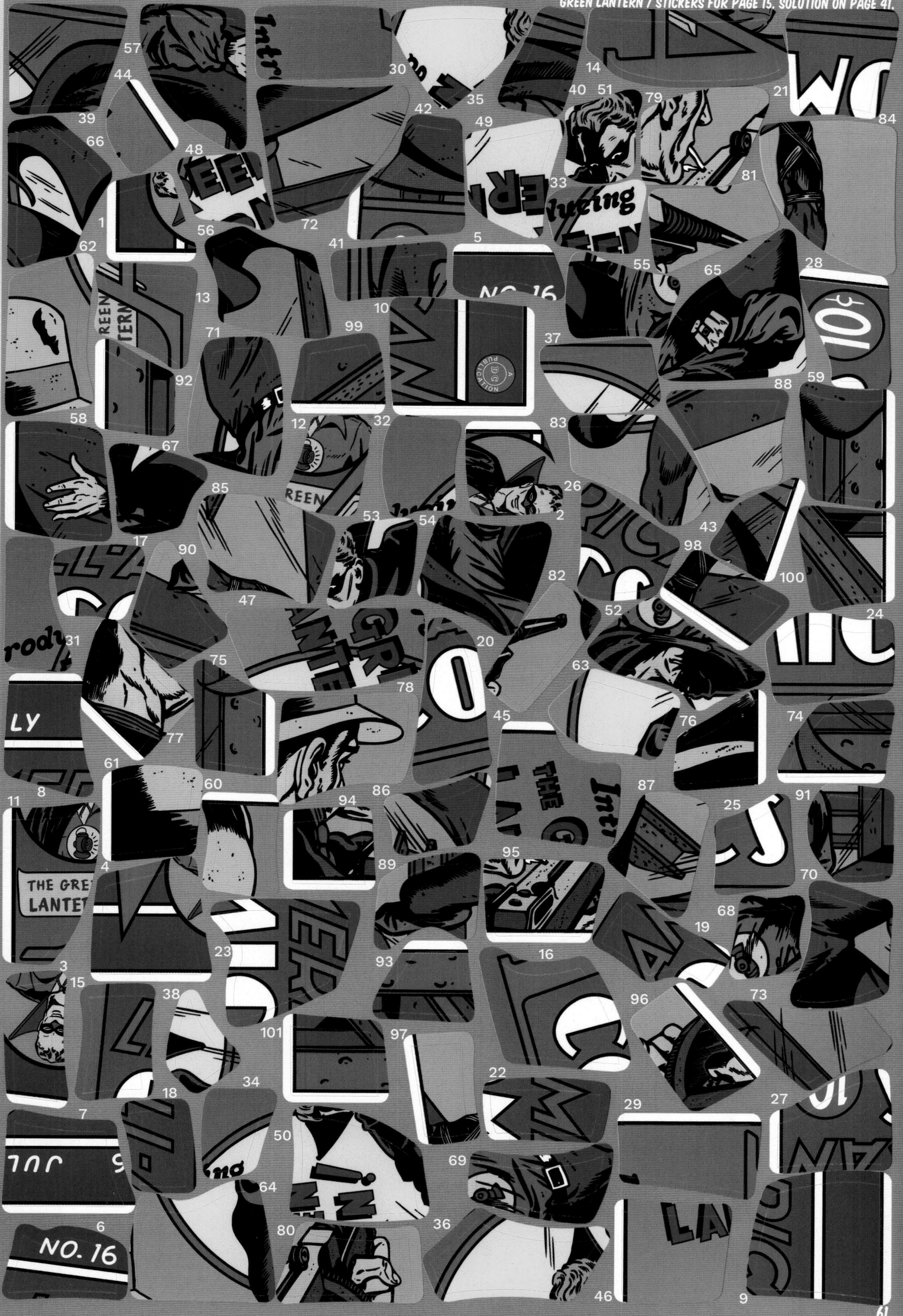
NO. 16
LY
THE GRE
LANTE
NO. 16

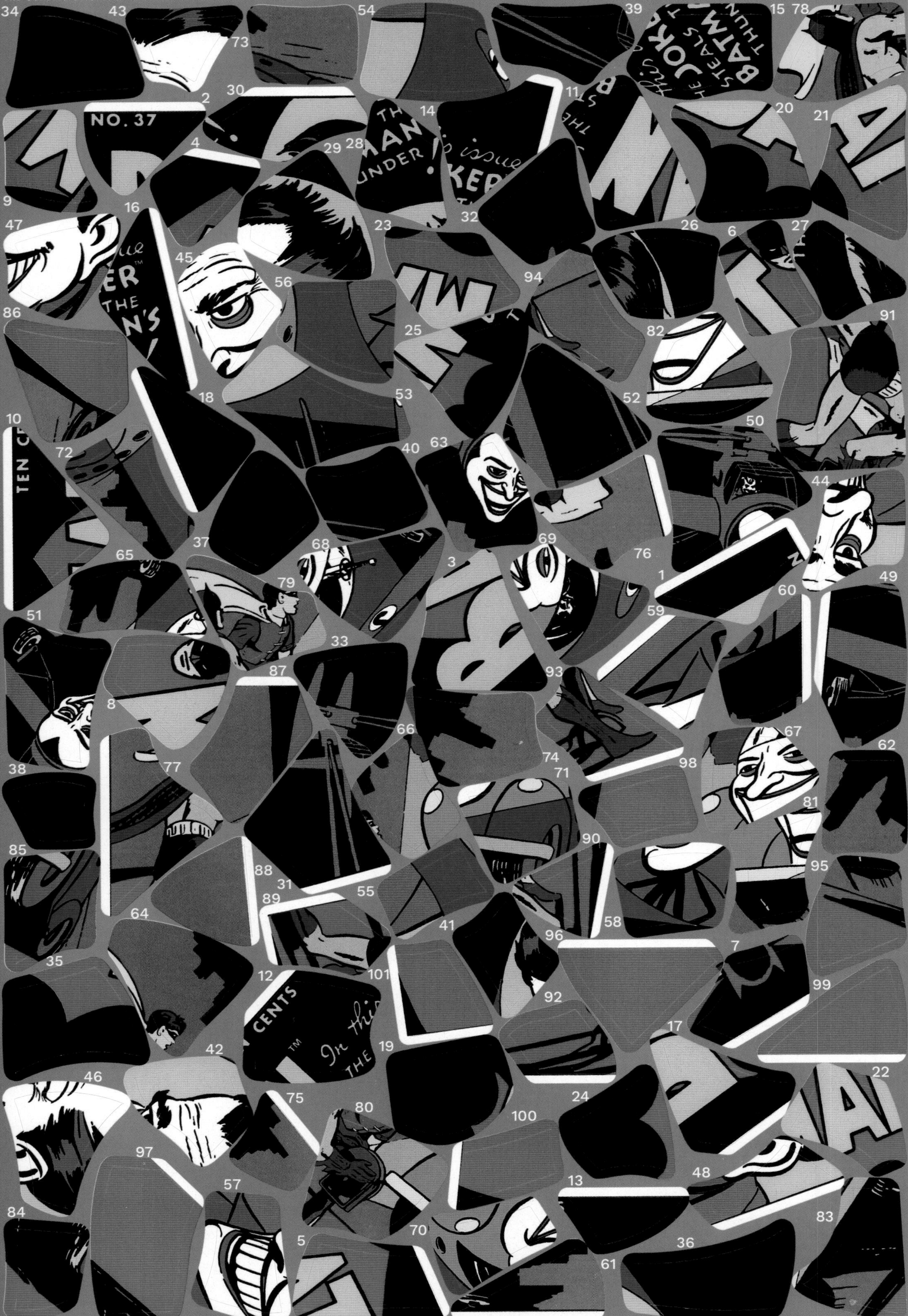
NO. 37
TEN C
CENTS

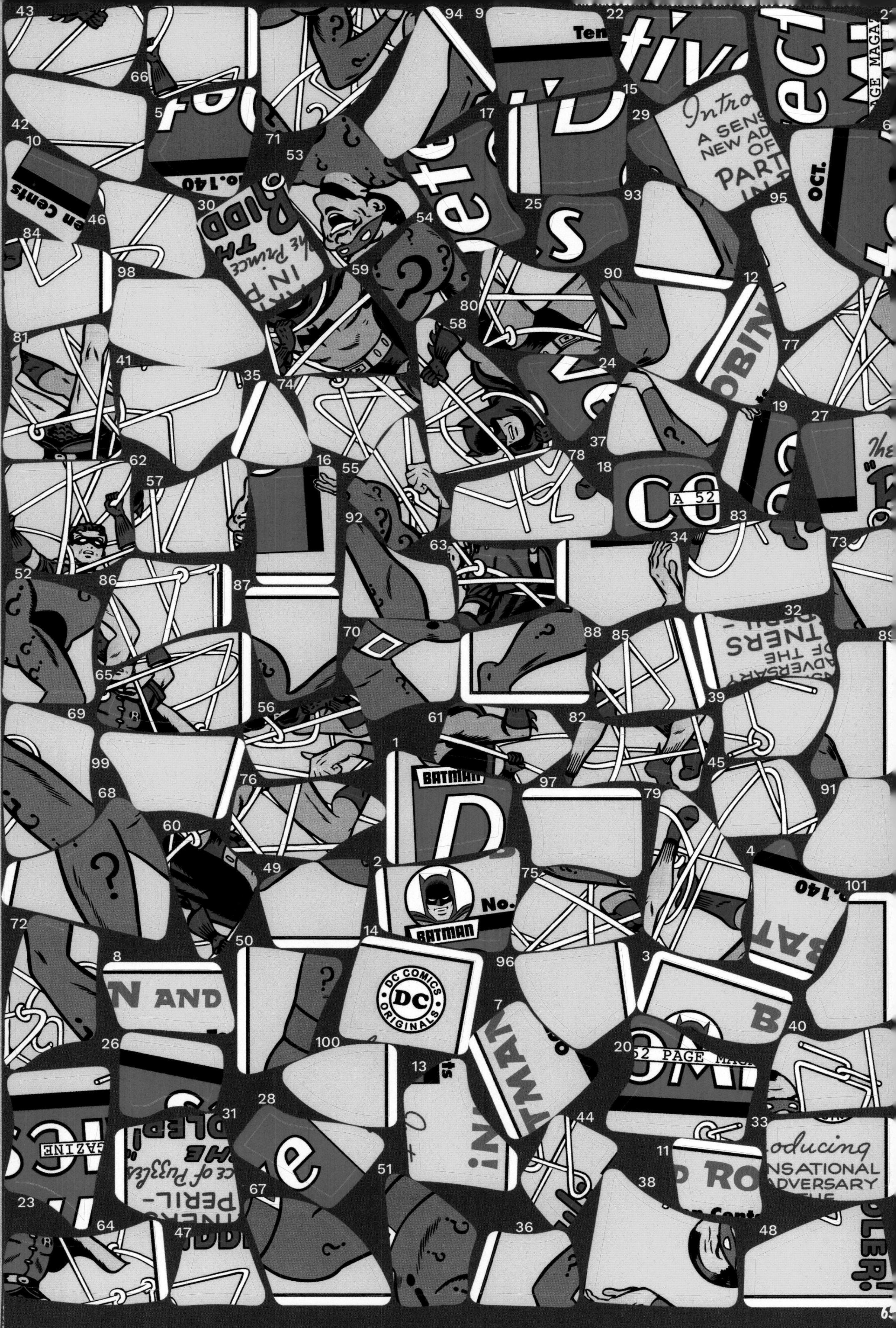
A 52
BATMAN
No.
BATMAN
DC COMICS ORIGINALS
N AND
52 PAGE MAGA
NSATIONAL
ADVERSARY
TNERS
OF THE
ADVERSARY
OCT.

CATWOMAN / STICKERS FOR PAGE 21. SOLUTION ON PAGE 44.

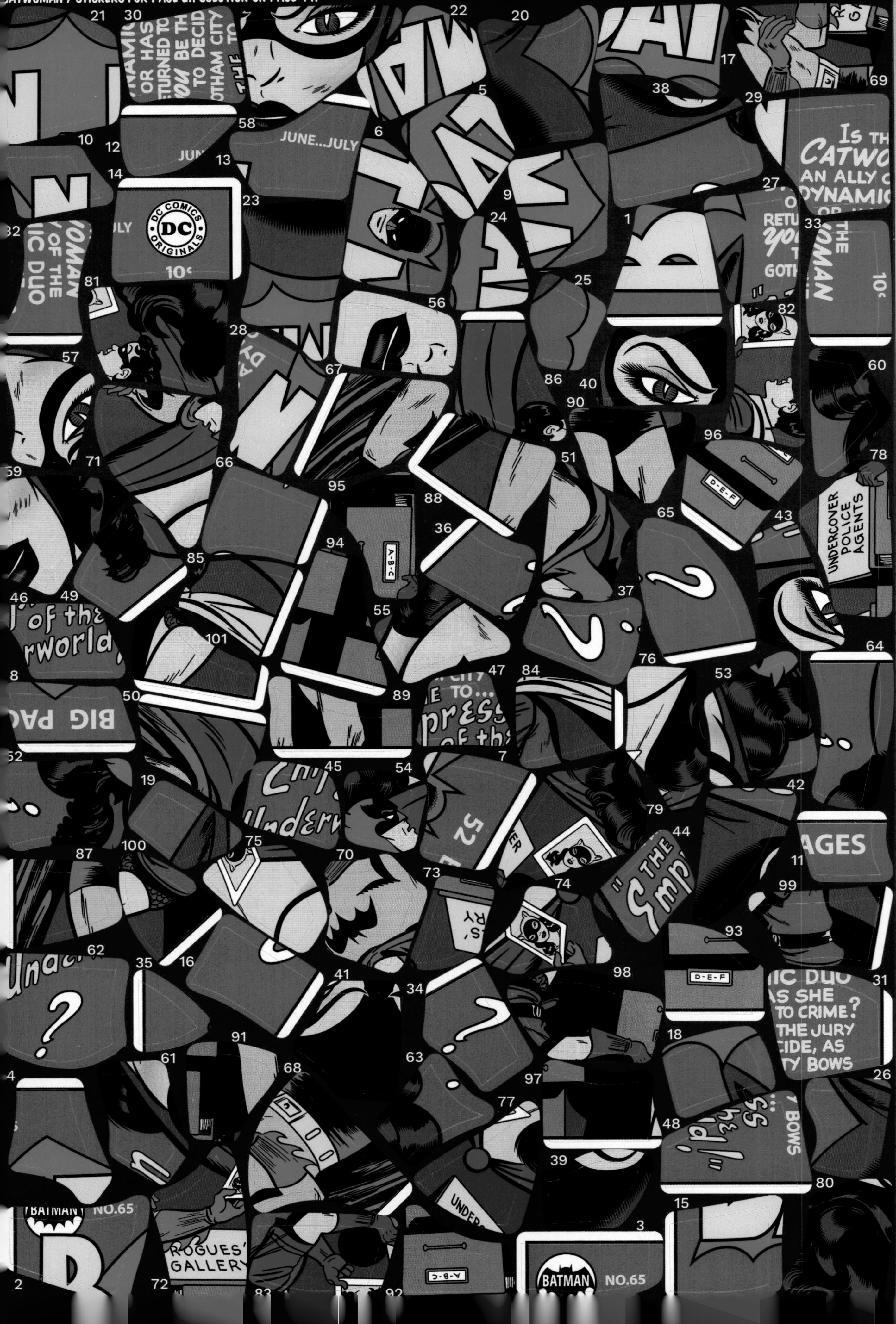

OR HAS
TURNED TO
YOU BE TH
TO DECID
OTHAM CITY
JUNE...JULY
JUN
DC COMICS ORIGINALS
10¢
Is THE
CATWO
AN ALLY O
DYNAMIC
RETU
YOU
GOTH
OF THE
IC DUO
THE
MAN
of the
rworld
BIG PAG
UNDERCOVER POLICE AGENTS
A-B-C
D-E-F
press
of th
Underw
AGES
THE
Emp
?
IC DUO
AS SHE
TO CRIME?
THE JURY
CIDE, AS
TY BOWS
BOWS
BATMAN NO.65
ROGUES' GALLERY
UNDER

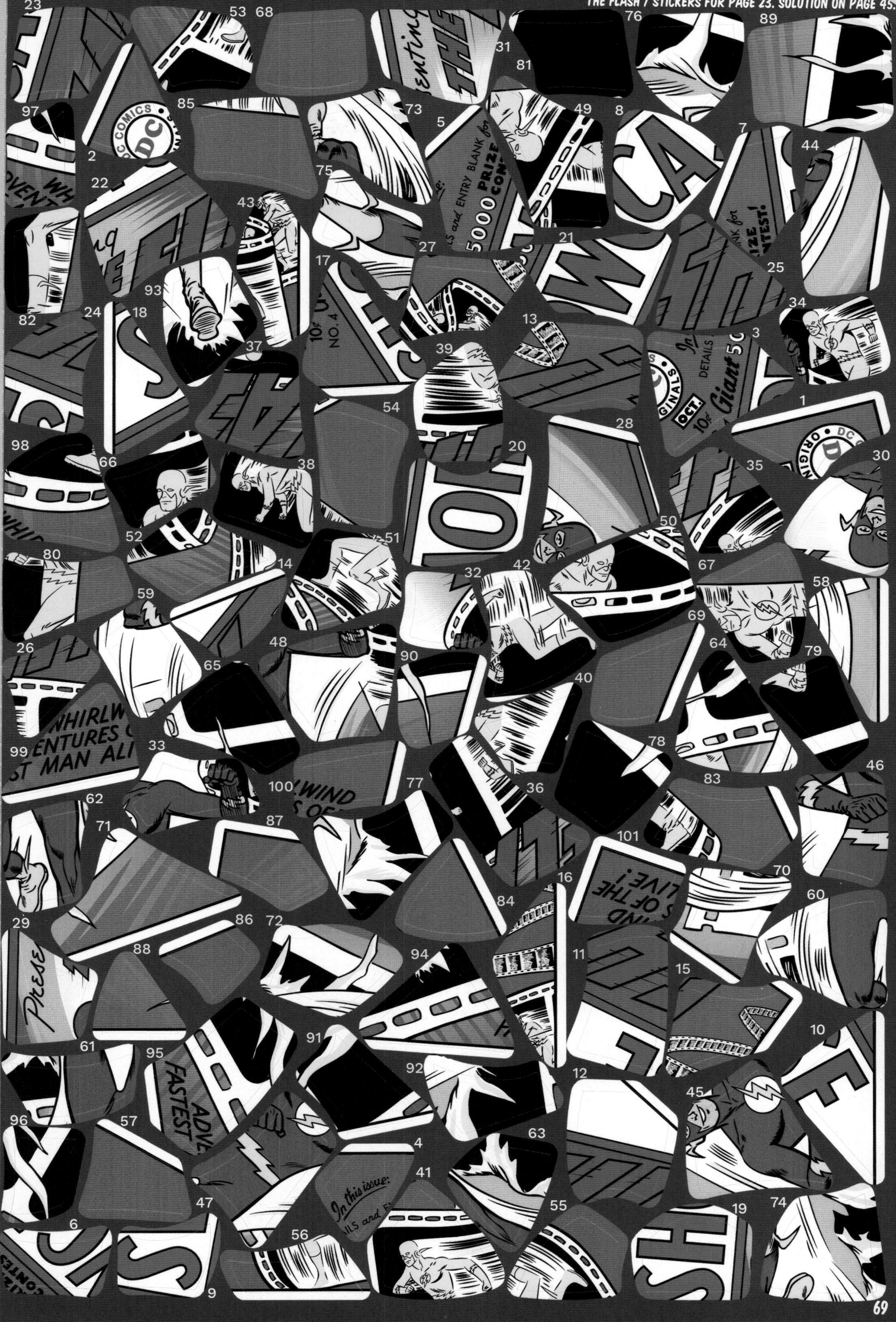
DC COMICS
ENTRY BLANK for
PRIZE CONT
5000
NO. 4
DETAILS
OCT.
10¢ Giant
WHIRLW
ENTURES
ST MAN ALI
WIND
S OF
LIVE!
FASTEST
ADV
In this issue:
PRESE

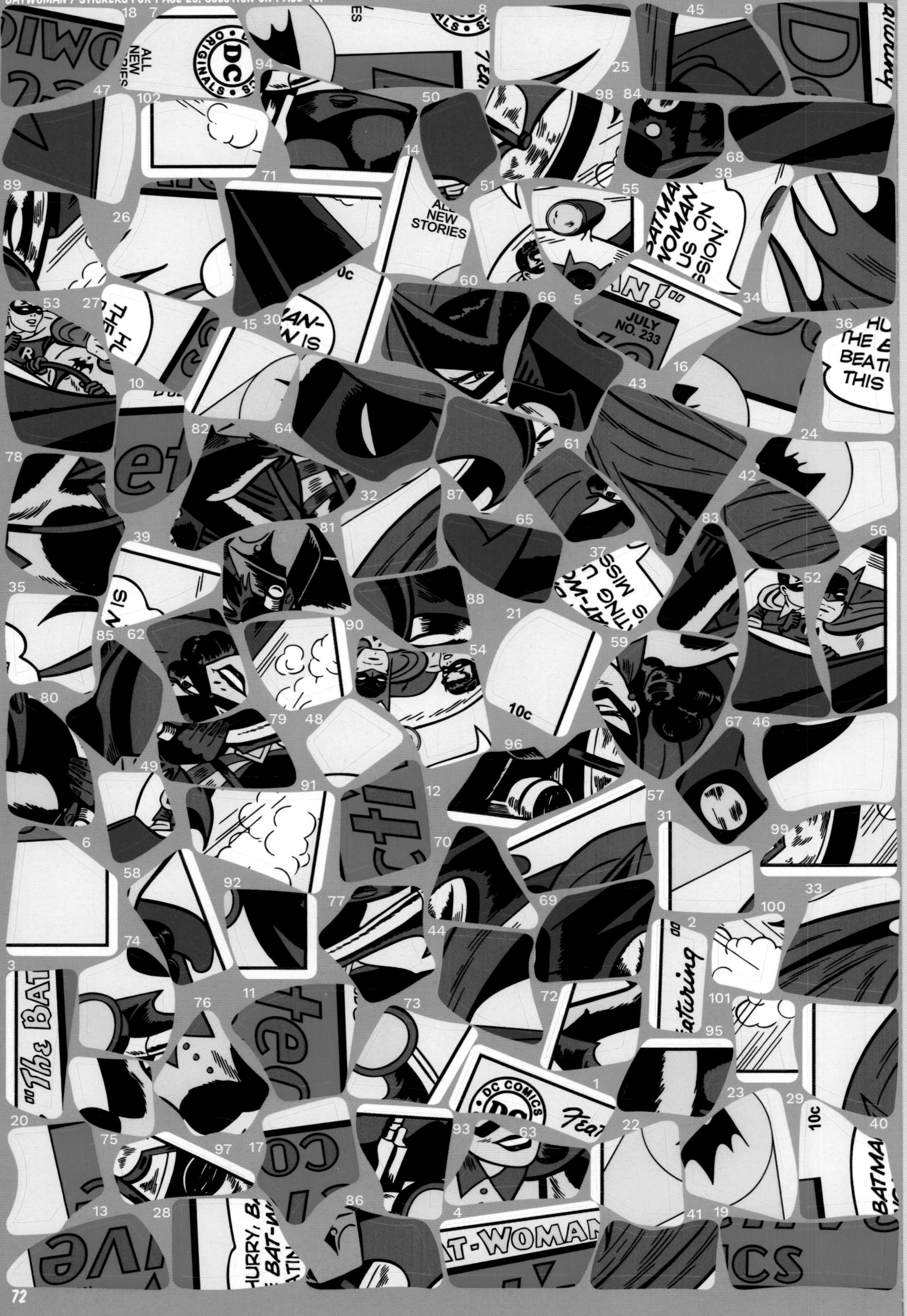
ALL NEW STORIES
DC ORIGINALS
JULY NO. 233
10c
DC COMICS
BAT-WOMAN

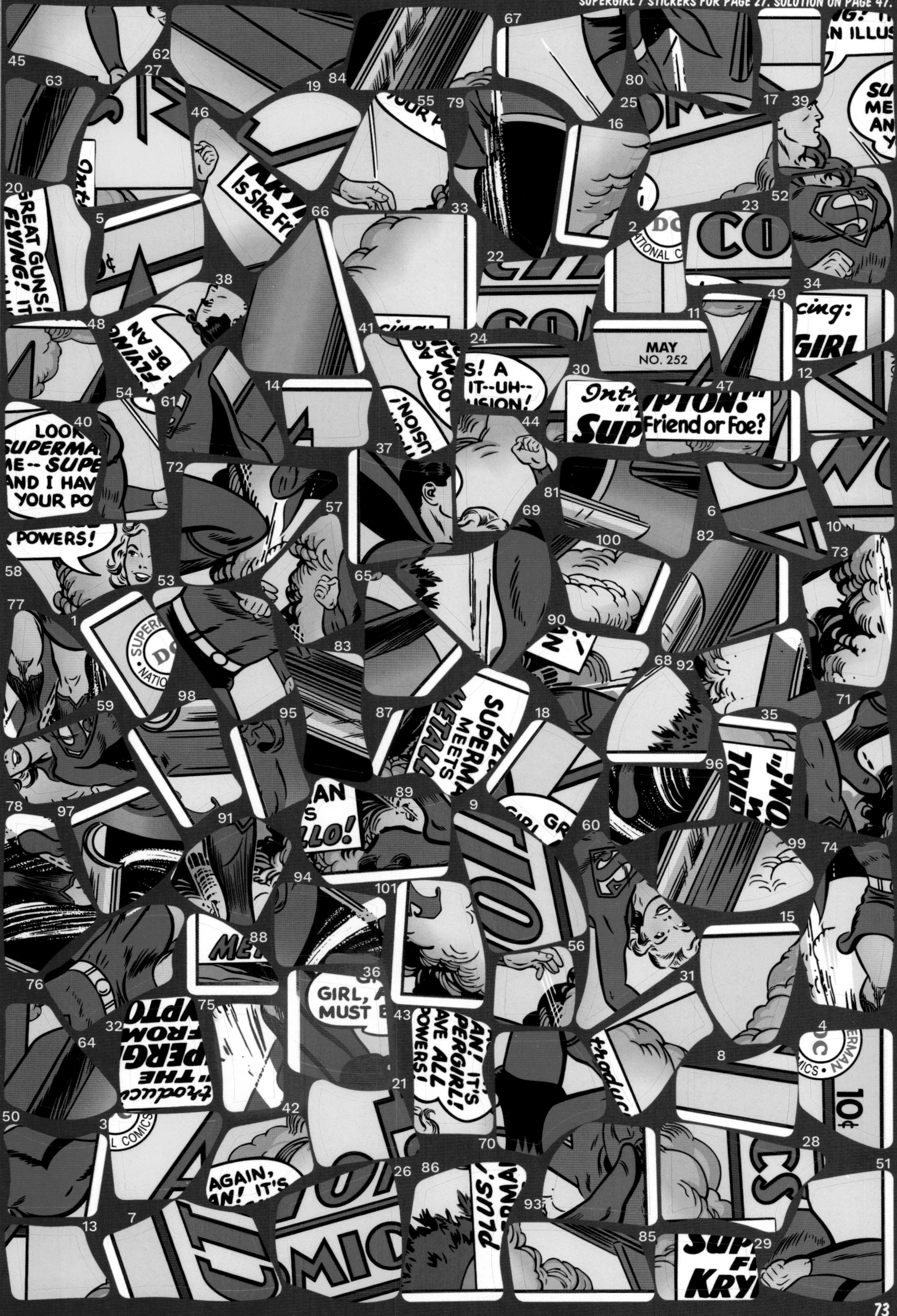
Is She Fr
GREAT GUNS!
FLYING!
MAY
NO. 252
Friend or Foe?
POWERS!
SUPERMAN MEETS
AGAIN,
ALL
COMICS

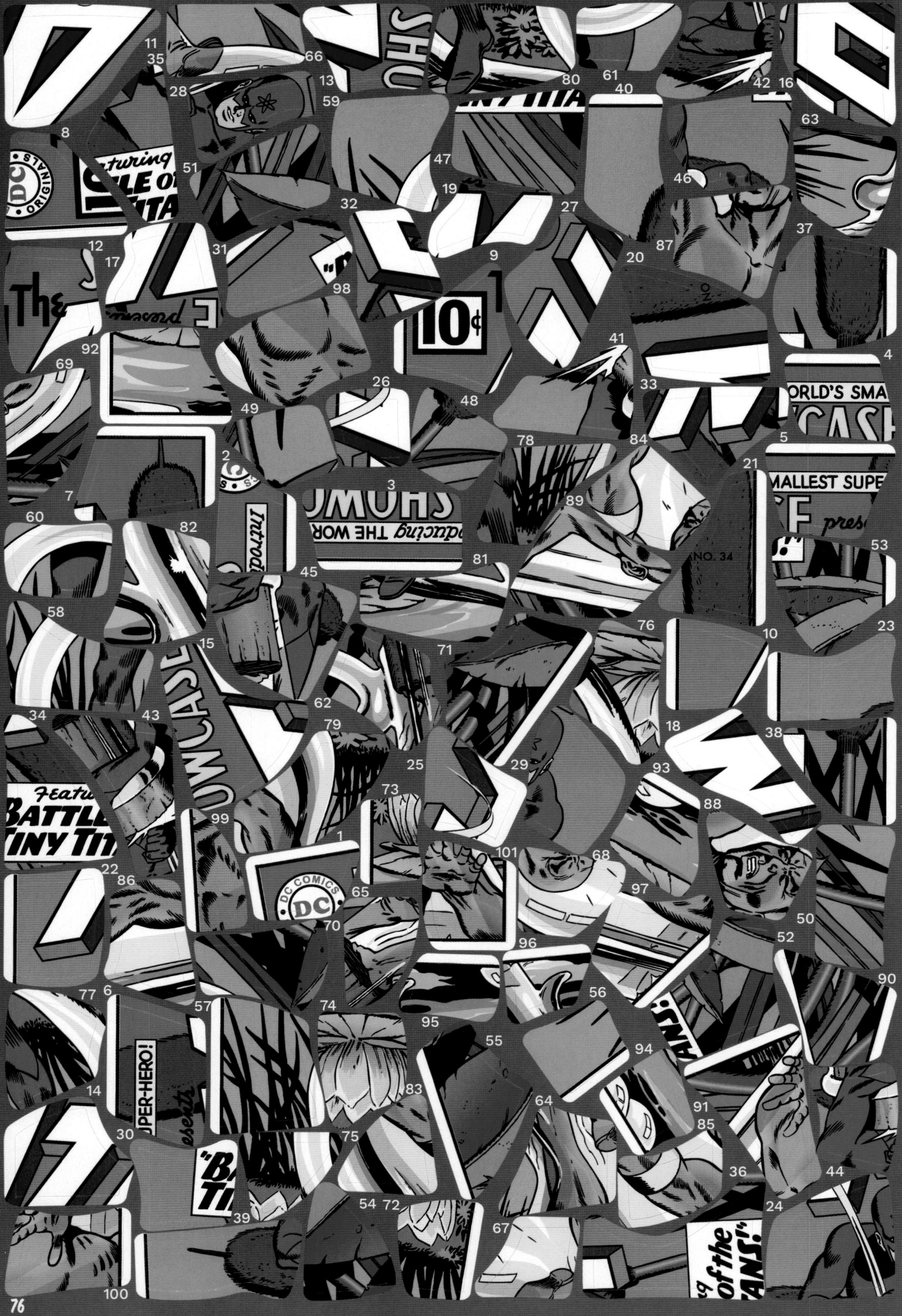
10¢
ORLD'S SMA
MALLEST SUPE
NO. 34
DC COMICS
SUPER-HERO!
Introducing THE WOR

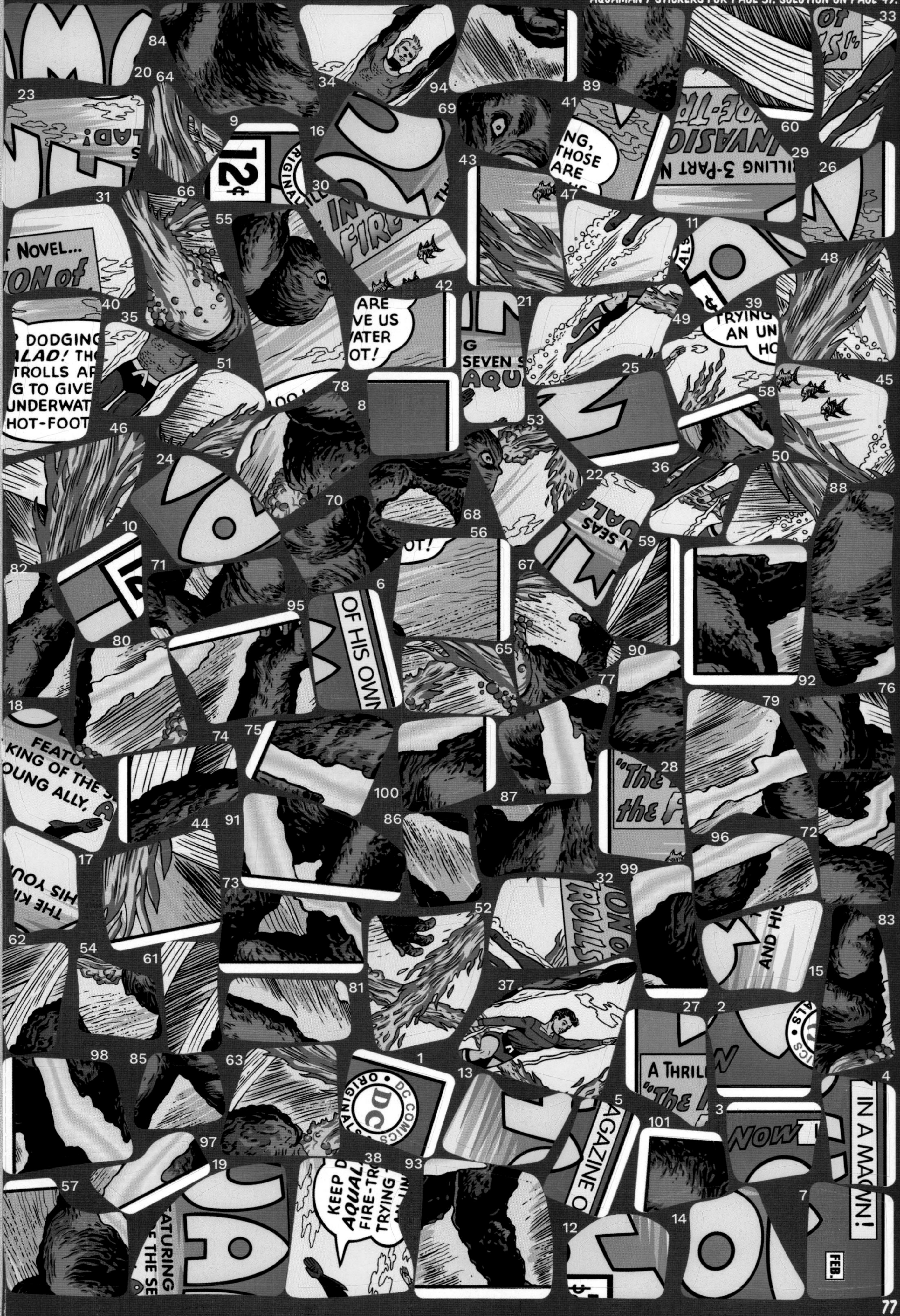

HAWKMAN / STICKERS FOR PAGE 33. SOLUTION ON PAGE 50.

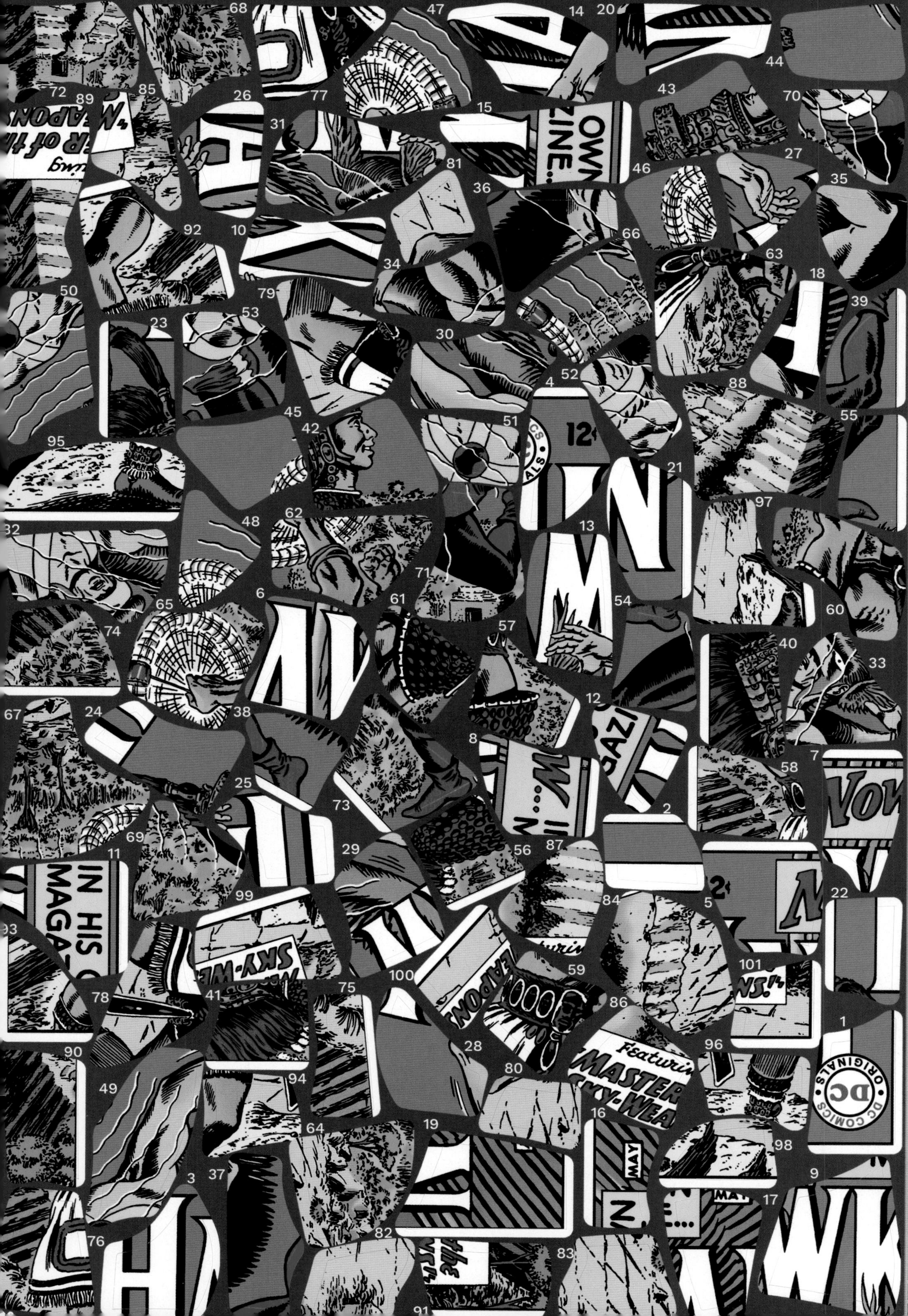

IN HIS
MAGA-
SKY-WE
Featuring
MASTER
SKY-WEA
12¢
DC COMICS ORIGINALS
MAY

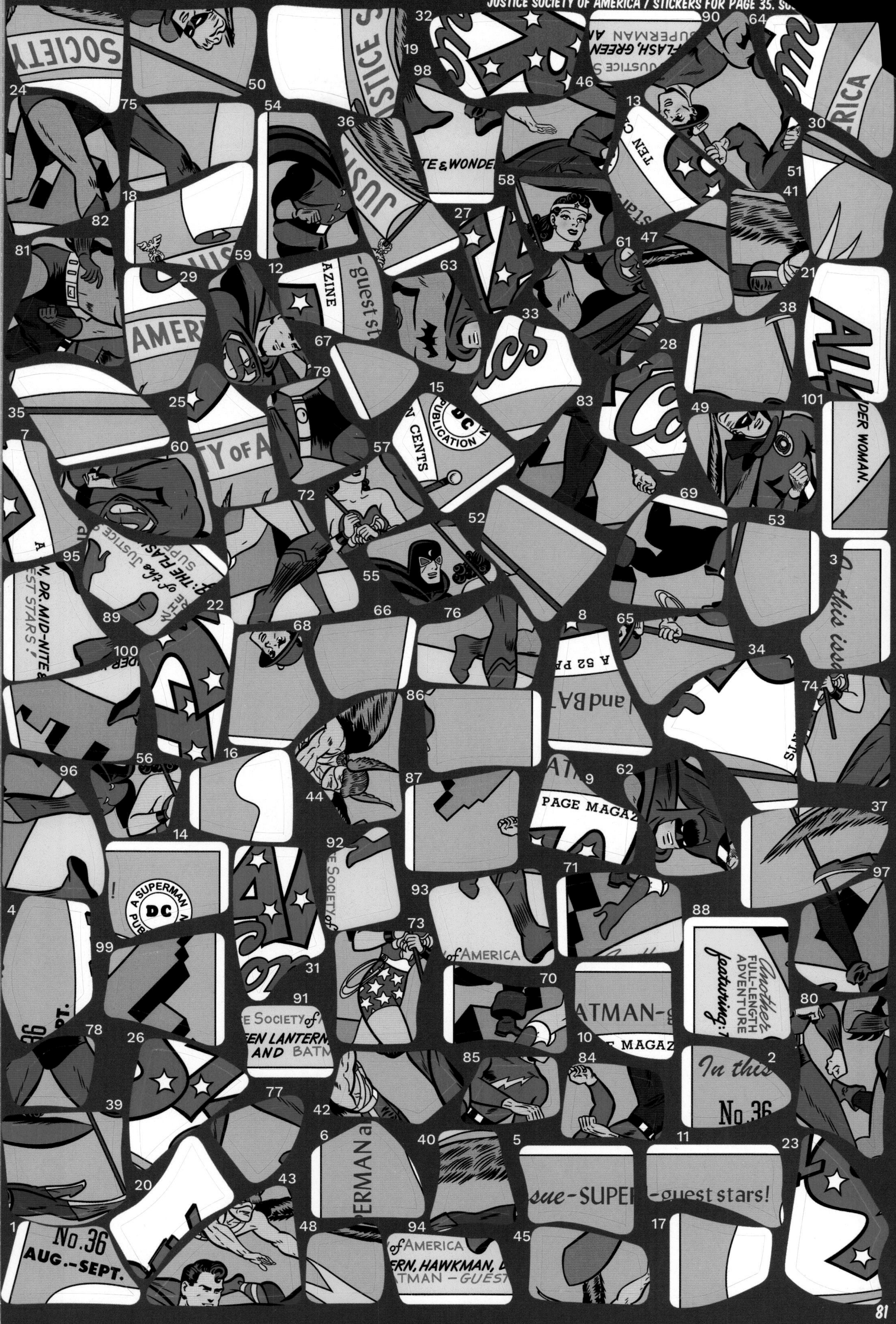
SOCIETY
JUSTICE S
TE & WONDE
AMER
-guest st
TY OF A
N CENTS
DC PUBLICATION
DER WOMAN.
A 52 PA
and BAT
PAGE MAGAZ
A SUPERMAN
DC
of AMERICA
E SOCIETY of A
EEN LANTERN,
AND BATM
ATMAN-g
E MAGAZ
Another FULL-LENGTH ADVENTURE featuring:
In this
No.36
ERMAN a
sue-SUPER-guest stars!
No.36
AUG.-SEPT.
of AMERICA
ERN, HAWKMAN, D
ATMAN – GUEST

SOLUTION ON PAGE 51.